HARVEST BELLS

HARVEST BELLS

New and Uncollected Poems

JOHN BETJEMAN

Edited and introduced by
Kevin J. Gardner

BLOOMSBURY CONTINUUM
LONDON · OXFORD · NEW YORK · NEW DELHI · SYDNEY

BLOOMSBURY CONTINUUM
Bloomsbury Publishing Plc
50 Bedford Square, London, WC1B 3DP, UK

BLOOMSBURY, BLOOMSBURY CONTINUUM and the Diana logo are
trademarks of Bloomsbury Publishing Plc

First published in Great Britain 2019

A catalogue record for this book is available from the British Library

Library of Congress Cataloguing-in-Publication data has been applied for

ISBN: HB: 978-1-4729-6638-4; ePDF: 978-1-4729-6640-7; ePUB: 978-1-4729-6639-1

2 4 6 8 10 9 7 5 3 1

Typeset by Integra Software Services Pvt. Ltd.
Printed and bound in Great Britain by CPI Group (UK) Ltd, Croydon CR0 4YY

To find out more about our authors and books visit www.bloomsbury.com and sign
up for our newsletters

I seem to have lost some of my manuscript poems as yet unpublished, or rather the typescripts of them.

John Betjeman
Letter to Jock Murray
7 December 1965

CONTENTS

PREFACE

This compilation of uncollected and previously unpublished poetry by John Betjeman aims to generate a deeper appreciation of the artistry and originality of England's best-loved twentieth-century poet. Beyond the recently resurrected poems that fill the pages of *Harvest Bells* are literally hundreds of Betjeman manuscripts waiting to be explored and studied. A scholarly study of his unfinished poems could generate a significantly richer understanding of his imagination than we have currently achieved. There is much work yet to be done toward a full appreciation of Betjeman's poetry, so it is my hope that this small selection of his less familiar verse will open that door.

Although this book is the result of more than ten years of archival research, it would not have been possible without the indefatigable scholarship of three bibliographers who forged the path toward the recovery of Betjeman's lost and overlooked poems. Genuinely ground-breaking work was done by Peter Gammond and John Heald in *A Bibliographical Companion to Betjeman* (The Betjeman Society, 1997), and in their revised and expanded edition, *Sir John Betjeman, 1906–1984: A Checklist of Writings by and about Him* (The Betjeman Society, 2005). Both volumes were instrumental to me in identifying Betjeman's uncollected periodical publications, particularly his juvenilia. But the recovery of Betjeman's unpublished poems is due largely to the heroic labours of William S. Peterson and his *John Betjeman: A Bibliography* (Clarendon Press, 2006). This immense catalogue inventories the contents of Betjeman manuscript archives across the United Kingdom and North America and is the richest compilation of his published and unpublished work to date.

In many respects the tireless toil of Gammond, Heald and Peterson is built on the bedrock of Bevis Hillier's monumental biography of Betjeman in three volumes: *Young Betjeman* (John Murray, 1988), *John Betjeman: New Fame, New Love* (John Murray, 2002) and *Betjeman: The Bonus of Laughter* (John Murray, 2004). Hillier's narrative of the life of Betjeman was an invaluable resource for dating poems and identifying references and is thus the foundation of this book. Also vital in this regard was Candida Lycett Green's superb edition of her father's correspondence, *Letters, Volume One: 1926–1951* (Methuen, 1994) and *Letters, Volume Two: 1951–1984* (Methuen, 1995). Having had Gammond and Heald, Peterson, Hillier and Lycett Green as my *vade mecums* throughout my research for this book, I remain in awe of their extraordinary scholarly achievements.

Of all the acknowledgements I must make, the most essential is to the family and estate of Sir John Betjeman for permission to pursue this research and to publish the poems in this volume. I would also like to thank Clare Alexander and Steph Adam of Aitken Alexander, who represented the Betjeman Estate. I have many people to thank at Bloomsbury, especially publishing director Robin Baird-Smith, who published three of my previous books (*Faith and Doubt of John Betjeman*, *Poems in the Porch: The Radio Poems of John Betjeman* and *Building Jerusalem: Elegies on Parish Churches*). I am especially grateful to the editing and production team at Bloomsbury, including my editor Jamie Birkett, copyeditor Richard Mason, proofreader Steve Cox and publicist Jude Drake.

A number of individuals offered advocacy, assistance or encouragement in my pursuit of this publication, namely Bevis Hillier, John R. and Virginia Murray, John Heald, Horace Liberty, Stephen Games, Roger Pringle, Anthony Thwaite, Peter Scupham, Andrew Motion, John Greening and Micheal O'Siadhail. To each of them I am grateful for their belief in this project, at times spurring me to persist when I despaired that I could ever bring it off. Their support sustained me on several occasions when my confidence wavered and I was tempted to throw in the towel. Perhaps most vital of all in this regard was my publisher Robin Baird-Smith, who urged me on in this project and kept my spirits up with his charm and wit. This book is my thanks to him for the long and jolly lunch at a Bloomsbury trattoria that inspired me to return to this project after a lengthy hiatus.

The staffs of numerous archives and libraries deserve accolades of praise and an endless stream of gratitude. Without the essential assistance of the following archivists, curators, keepers, librarians and researchers, this book would surely not have been possible: Michael Basinski, James Maynard and Alison Fraser (University Libraries, The State University of New York at Buffalo); Anne Mouron (Bodleian Library, University of Oxford); Terry Tuey and John Frederick (McPherson Library, University of Victoria); Anne Marie Menta and Rebecca Aldi (Beinecke Rare Book and Manuscript Library, Yale University); Chido Uchemwa and Teresa Loyd (Harry Ransom Center, University of Texas); John R. and

Virginia Murray (John Murray Archives); Isaac Gewirtz and Anne Garner (Berg Collection, New York Public Library); Charlotte Berry and Ben Taylor (Magdalen College Archives, University of Oxford); Judith Curthoys (Christ Church Archives, University of Oxford); Sue Inskip (Special Collections, University of Exeter); Matt Dunne and Helen Price (Brotherton Library, University of Leeds); Sally Jennings (Eton College Library); T. E. Rogers (Marlborough College Archives); and the anonymous staff members of the British Library (Betjeman Archive and Document Supply Service).

Numerous other kind souls answered my endless emails, often pertaining to elusive Betjeman manuscripts and allusions in his poems, and I would be remiss in not thanking them for their generosity of time and effort: Lisa Brophy (Foyles Bookshop); Christian Algar (British Library Newspapers); Donna Derbyshire (Telegraph Media Group); Martin Steenson (Books & Things); Rachel Beattie and Kristy McHugh (National Library of Scotland); David Frasier (Lilly Library, Indiana University); Bruce Hunter (David Higham Associates); Jeffrey Hackney (Wadham College Archives, University of Oxford); Amy Boylan (Balliol College Library, University of Oxford); Mark Bainbridge (Worcester College Library, University of Oxford); Amanda Ingram (Pembroke College Archives, University of Oxford); Julian Reid (Merton College Archives, University of Oxford); Catherine Sutherland (Magdalene College Library, University of Cambridge); H. C. Carron and Amanda Goode (Emmanuel College Library and Archives, University of Cambridge); Louise Hughes (Special Collections and Archives, University of Gloucestershire); C. S. Knighton (Clifton College Archives); Katie Barrett (Cheltenham College Archives); Matt Bazley (Northamptonshire Record Office); Patrick Perry (Estate of Lionel Perry); Edward Peake (Sezincote House); William Offhaus (University Archives, The State University of New York at Buffalo); Tim Young (Beinecke Library, Yale University); Shane Taylor (Tarrington Books); Henry Hardy (Wolfson College, University of Oxford); Andy Wisely (Department of German, Baylor University); and the Revd Canon Dana Delap (Church of St Lawrence, Bourton-on-the-Hill).

Finally, I offer my greatest thanks to my family, who have long endured my pursuit of white rabbits. I am entirely grateful to them for keeping me securely grounded. To Hilary, my wife, and Graham, my son, this volume is dedicated.

INTRODUCTION

John Betjeman's ten individual books of poetry, and
the single collected volume that comprises them, repre-
sent fifty years of a fertile and unique imagination.[1] His
unforgettable poems on landscape and suburbia, desire
and death, faith and doubt, helped to establish him as the
beloved voice of a nation. Yet the 223 pieces that make up
Collected Poems are an incomplete representation of his
poetic output. Many poems that he published in maga-
zines and newspapers were excluded from his books,
and a substantial number of completed poems were
never printed at all. This was not a reflection of authorial
intent or the quality of the poems but rather the result
of Betjeman's frenzied work schedule, misguided advice
from his literary advisers, and careless filing and chaotic
organizational practices. The recovery of his uncollected
and unpublished poems gives new and essential insight
into his poetic imagination and habits as a writer. We are
only just beginning to understand the complexities of
Betjeman's vision; thus the recovery of his lost works is
sure to create not only an expanded canon of his poetry
but also a deeper and more nuanced appreciation of his
mind.

The map to discovering Betjeman's lost poetry is sketched in the pre-publication history of his books. The narratives painstakingly unfolded by biographer Bevis Hillier and bibliographer William S. Peterson reveal a pattern of suppression and neglect. A recurring thread is the poet's tendency to rely on others for significant editorial and authorial decisions. This was due in part to the occupational demands of his print and broadcast journalism commitments, which severely limited the time needed for such considerations. But there was also the fact that his publisher John Grey 'Jock' Murray, and his literary advisers Peter Quennell, John Sparrow, Tom Driberg and Freddie Birkenhead, had very strong opinions that were sometimes difficult to budge. Debate over their contents characterized almost every volume Murray published, and Betjeman rarely resisted or asserted control. Perhaps only with his first book, *Mount Zion* – significantly, his sole book of poems not published by Murray – was there no collaborative interference, yet nearly half its contents were excluded from *Collected Poems*.

Murray himself was always involved, sometimes quite substantially, in what to include or exclude. He and Betjeman made frequent changes to the titles and contents of books right up until they went to press, and the initial selection of poems was often given to Betjeman's long-time friends.[2] Even for his final volumes, *High and Low* and *A Nip in the Air*, published at the height of his success and popularity, Betjeman resigned primary control over the contents to Birkenhead and Driberg, and he granted full selection of the contents of *Uncollected Poems* to his biographer.[3] For

1948's *Selected Poems*, Hillier reports that John Sparrow functioned as 'ringmaster', exercising 'absolute control' over everything from choice of contents to the format of the edition. He rejected not only the author's preference for a cheap, popular edition but also the publisher's preference for a large and representative selection of verse, asserting to Murray, 'We both agreed vehemently that what would be best . . . is a comparatively small selection of his really good poetry. We also agreed on which were his best poems.'[4]

For 'we', read 'I': if Betjeman agreed, it was because he trusted Sparrow more than himself. It is not the case that he didn't have strong opinions, merely that he sometimes allowed himself to be vetoed because he did not sufficiently value his own judgement. As a *Collected Poems* was being discussed, Murray informed the poet that a 'collected' edition would not necessarily include every poem published, which implied to Betjeman, perhaps more disparagingly than was intended, that someone 'would have to separate the wheat from the chaff'.[5] Yet when the final selections were being made, Murray wrote that this volume 'should include those poems which you can be persuaded not to feel embarrassed to see in print'.[6] This only reinforced a tendency in Betjeman to derogate his own work; he suggested, for instance, that Bevis Hillier use 'Barrel Scrapings' as a title for *Uncollected Poems*.[7] An oft-quoted passage from a 1938 letter to Charles Abbott (a figure who reappears later in this narrative), in which Betjeman describes his process of composition, suggests that self-deprecation was not merely a humorous defence mechanism but a genuine lack of self-assurance: 'I generally write on the backs of envelopes & in flyleaves of cheap books & gather the material together – generally all in one day. Then I type the thing out & look at it the next morning, think its [*sic*]very bad & forget about it & it gets lost. This happens to much that I write in verse.'[8] Here in this nutshell of diffidence and carelessness we sense why a good bit of Betjeman's poetry never saw the light of day.

Further complicating the problem was Betjeman's curious inattention to record-keeping. Murray quickly learned that it would be his own responsibility to maintain an account of the poems printed in periodicals as well as those not yet published, and to develop and coordinate a meticulous process of revision and review. Hillier's perspective on the production of *High and Low* is particularly illustrative. He drily recounts, 'The usual process began, by which secretaries rummaged through desk drawers and magazine editors were plagued for lists of the Betjeman poems they had published in the last few years.'[9] Betjeman himself compounded the problem with his carelessness; in 1965 he wrote to Murray as preparations were under way, 'I seem to have lost some of my manuscript poems as yet unpublished, or rather the typescripts of them. I would be very grateful if you could have typed out and sent to me a complete collection of my unpublished publishable verse. I may take a look at it with a view to writing more and filling gaps.'[10]

Despite the valiant efforts of Betjeman's publisher, advisers and secretaries to keep track of what he had written and what he had published, numerous pieces eluded them. William Peterson, who has done more than anyone since Bevis Hillier to sort out the chaos, reminds us that it was not merely a personal aversion to orderliness that accounted for the chaos of Betjeman's literary records, and it could certainly not be attributed to laziness: 'Betjeman himself was too busy writing – at a pace that amazed his friends and family – to have any time to document the large paper trail he was leaving behind him.'[11] For literary detectives, manuscripts of Betjeman's unpublished but publishable verse may not quite measure up to the Lost Library of the Moscow Tsars, but to Betjephiles such a discovery is nonetheless tantalizing.

BETJEMAN IN THE ARCHIVES

Betjeman's unpublished poems survive today in various archives across the United Kingdom and North America. In 1971 Betjeman sold sixteen boxes of his personal papers to the McPherson Library at the University of Victoria, a collection that has since grown to eighty-five boxes and twenty-four metres of shelf space containing diaries, account books, page proofs, typescripts, manuscripts, worksheets, notebooks and an estimated 50,000 pieces of individual correspondence. It is by far the largest repository of Betjeman research materials in the world. When Bill Peterson was conducting research for his monumental bibliography, he found the collection had not yet been fully inventoried (though it has been since, in a 557-page catalogue), so it is unsurprising that he referred to it, not entirely unlovingly, as 'a bottomless pit'.[12] Peterson was the first bibliographer to record unpublished manuscripts by Betjeman. Perhaps my first hint that unpublished but publishable poems might exist was that he had catalogued no fewer than 677 individual poems – whereas only 223 appear in the *Collected Poems*. However, Peterson's number should not be taken as a final tally, nor did he intend it to be: some individually catalogued drafts are unidentified versions of the same poem;

many of the catalogue poems are mere fragments; and still other poems have not yet been identified.

In addition to the massive collection at Victoria, substantial archives of Betjeman materials are deposited in the British Library (a compilation of three collections once belonging to publisher Jock Murray, to American collector H. Bradley Martin, and to Betjeman's daughter Candida Lycett Green); in the Beinecke Library at Yale University (formed from the private collection of bibliophile Duncan Andrews); in the University of Exeter's Special Collections (which holds Betjeman's personal library as well as some manuscript materials); in the John Murray Archives in London (which has correspondence concerning Betjeman's publication history and an impressive collection of poetry manuscripts); and in the Harry Ransom Center at the University of Texas (which holds a sizeable number of prose manuscripts and letters as well as some poetry). Smaller gatherings are in the Berg Collection at the New York Public Library, the Brotherton Library at the University of Leeds, the Magdalen College, Oxford, Archives, and the Bodleian Library. A handful of manuscripts – mostly correspondence – is also scattered among archives in schools, colleges and universities across the United Kingdom.

While all sorts of manuscripts of Betjeman's are preserved in these archives and libraries, by far the most concentrated trove of his poetic manuscripts is deposited in the Poetry Collection in the University Libraries at The State University of New York at Buffalo. Charles D. Abbott, a former Rhodes Scholar at New College, Oxford, began the Poetry Collection at Buffalo in 1935, soon after his appointment as Director of University

Libraries. In addition to amassing the world's largest collection of poetry first editions and little literary magazines published in English after 1900, Abbott also determined to collect manuscripts and letters of living poets. Years later, he recalled: 'We needed manuscripts if we were to help the scholar in his struggle to penetrate towards the core of the puzzle ... All the tangible papers that a poet uses in making a poem. Something like that might give the theorist real bricks and mortar. Even if the nebulous inception of a poem could not be captured, the cerebral agitation that precedes the first act of writing, how vividly worksheets might unfold the course of labor, growth and change.'[13] He wrote to hundreds of poets asking for anything from drafts of poems to the contents of their bins, with a particular interest in the worksheets that could demonstrate the poet's creative process. 'Worksheets,' he mused. 'Every day hundreds were tossed to the wastebasket and the fire. Why not ask for them?'[14] When his letters proved only marginally successful, he decided to call on poets in person. He made his first visit to London in January 1938, staying for three months in a rented flat on Ebury Street and visiting nearly a hundred poets, perhaps even more.[15]

The Betjeman collection at Buffalo was formed in three distinct phases, starting in 1938 and ending in 1960. The final donation is easiest to date: in a letter to the collection's new curator, David Posner, Betjeman asked, 'Do you think the enclosed two fragments from my autobiography are worthy of the distinguished company which they will join in your Library?'[16] The earlier acquisitions are trickier to determine. While on his first trip to London, Charles Abbott met Betjeman; how this was arranged and where it occurred is uncertain, but Abbott and his wife regularly entertained poets in their flat. The surviving correspondence from Betjeman suggests that the meeting was quite early in Abbott's stay, and probably brief. On 10 March, Betjeman wrote to Abbott, enclosing two manuscript drafts; he expressed his gratitude, described his method of writing (quoted above), invited him to visit him in his office in London, and concluded with an apology for his delay in responding to Abbott's request: 'I am indeed flattered to be counted by you a poet of significance . . . I enclose for you here the only couple of rough drafts of poems I have written that I can find . . . The two drafts I enclose, – one on Exeter which I rather like – & one on Slough which I think is crude and poor – are, as far as I recollect, original draughts [*sic*] . . . I am to be found at Shell Mex House (Temple Bar 1234) on Mons, Tues & Weds each week from 11–4.30, if you w^d care to see me.'[17] Was there a reply from Abbott, perhaps a note of thanks and a farewell greeting? Two days later, on 12 March, Betjeman wrote to Abbott again, this time a brief postcard: 'Many thanks for your encouraging letter. Hope to see you when next you are over. I remember you quite well – you wore a green tie.'[18]

When was Abbott next over? No one knows, but most likely it was not long after the war, at which time he made off with an extraordinary pile of Betjeman's manuscripts. In addition to the first donation of drafts of 'Exeter' and 'Slough' and the final donation of fragments of *Summoned by Bells*, Abbott's collection at Buffalo holds manuscript drafts of approximately ninety Betjeman poems, including holograph drafts and typescripts of twenty-nine published poems; the remaining drafts are

8

of at least sixty original poems of Betjeman's that have never appeared in print. Of these sixty-plus poems, more than half are inchoate fragments, but twenty or more are highly polished and complete works. The titles of some of the manuscript drafts of the twenty-nine published poems indicate that this major donation occurred after the war. While most of those were drafts of poems that had been published in *Mount Zion* (1931) and *Continual Dew* (1937), four appeared in *Old Lights for New Chancels* (1940) and three in *New Bats in Old Belfries* (1945). Additionally, the Buffalo collection contains a letter from Jock Murray to Betjeman, dated 20 November 1939, with questions pertaining to the production of *Old Lights*, on the verso of which is a working draft of 'Bristol and Clifton': Betjeman visited Bristol in 1940 to witness the bomb damage from the Luftwaffe and took inspiration from the city for this poem. All this evidence suggests that Abbott's largest acquisition of Betjeman manuscripts occurred post-1945. While a precise date cannot be ascertained, there is little doubt that Abbott's determination to build an archive of the poetic imagination at work preserved these master-pieces from certain oblivion in the dustbin or ash heap.[19]

HIDDEN MASTERPIECES

A question naturally arising in a project of this nature concerns the quality of the selections. I explain my prin-ciples of editorial selection in the next section of this introduction, thinking it sufficient here to state that all of the poems included in this volume have been subjected to rigorous scrutiny. Some are, admittedly, mere trifles: these, I would argue, are nevertheless elegant and charming bits of light verse that demonstrate poetic skill as much as the more tonally complicated pieces. Most important, however, is that in all instances these newly uncovered poems reveal new layers to Betjeman's imagination and creativity.

Much of his *Collected Poems* revels in the influences of Victorian poets, but here one may discover a number of unexpected influences. One of the most surprising is the Romantic poets. Percy Shelley in particular may seem an unlikely influence, with his lush imagery, overwrought emotion and atheism. However, as a youth Betjeman had a fairly extended agnostic phase, refusing confirmation while at Marlborough College and not rediscovering religion until he was at Oxford. Many of his early unpublished poems (for instance, 'Wisteria Branches' and 'Lerici 1930') have those poetic qualities associated with Romantic self-indulgence. At the same time they also demonstrate the 1920s taste, especially prominent at Oxford, for the florid and avant-garde verse of the Sitwells. Ultimately, Betjeman would find his natural voice in the forms and rhythms of the obscurer Victorian poets and hymnodists, but his early experimentation with Romanticism reveals a more complicated poet than we have heretofore appreciated – especially surprising from one who publicly expressed his dislike of Shelley.[20]

A well-known undercurrent of Betjeman's personality was a depressive streak. But many of the poems in this collection seem deeply fraught with anxiety about love and death. The playful rhythms and scenes of 'Emily Wren' give way to the horror of a sudden death. The easy comforts of church bells in the English countryside mask the heartbreak of infant death in 'Harvest Bells'. 'On Miss E. Badger' sees lust succumb to the imagined horrors of old age and the grave. Suicide is the only recourse for the financial victim of 'Big Business'. And the theological consolations of the Feast of All Saints are supplanted by assurances of eternal death in 'Clay and Spirit'. These poems offer an expansive understanding of Betjeman's darker moods, recounted in such familiar pieces from *Collected Poems* as 'Before the Anaesthetic', 'Late-Flowering Lust' and 'Five O'Clock Shadow'.

A further revelation about his personality can be found in this collection, which I hope serves as an antidote to an unfortunate myth about Betjeman's cuddliness. This myth, created in part through the author's many television appearances, was sealed in the public imagination when *The Times* labelled him 'teddy bear to the nation' in 1972.[21] Careful readers of Betjeman already know this image to be false, but few who work through this volume will come away with an amiable or jolly impression of the poet laureate. He revelled in indecency, as when he imagined the awkward encounters and sexual fumblings of cloistered public-school boys. He could be savage and relentless, not just to faceless urban planners, socialists and economy-minded bishops, but also to his friends. Subject to his satiric wit were his surrogate family, the Dugdales of Sezincote; early friends from Oxford and Marlborough such as Anthony Blunt, John Edward Bowle and Norman Cameron; and Oxford don and salon host Colonel Kolkhorst. Who knew that Betjeman had buried deep inside him the spirit of Alexander Pope? Underneath that cuddly exterior ran streaks of filth and malice.

Perplexingly, this savagery ran alongside a genuine vein of tolerance and gentleness. The same Betjeman who satirized spiritual excess in an 'Evangelical Hymn' could simultaneously imagine an evangelical Christian's 'Sudden Conversion' with forbearance and dignity. This is a Betjeman who could see his England simultaneously from two conflicting perspectives, who (in the year 1946, for instance) could write one poem joyfully celebrating the recovery of Margate after the destruction of the war, and another bitterly embracing the inevitable loss of this same England to socialists ('Margate, 1946' and 'A Memory of 1940'). There is no doubt that this is a poet much more complicated than he is often allowed to be. The Betjeman revealed in the pages of *Harvest Bells* is of course the same Betjeman we all know from *Collected Poems*, but an immersion in his lost work gives us a deeper and more nuanced understanding of this enigmatic poet, often bewildering but always pleasing.

EDITORIAL PRINCIPLES

Editing a volume of this nature is an extraordinarily difficult task. By far the most onerous decision is the one earlier faced by Betjeman's own friends and literary advisers – what to include and what to exclude. For example, a dilemma arises when faced with pieces that might not have been finished, or were designed for a specific public occasion, or that seem highly personal in character: a strong justification to include would be needed in such instances. I found my sympathy for John Sparrow and Tom Driberg expanding while I worked on this volume. The first principle was that this was not to be a complete edition of Betjeman's poetry. A complete edition would include all published poems, no matter how ephemeral, occasional, or personal, as well as all unpublished poems, even fragments and unpolished drafts. Instead, my intention was to select the best of Betjeman's poetry that for a variety of reasons, largely explored above, has heretofore been uncollected or excluded from print. Out of well more than 150 possibilities, I selected for this book perhaps half of those, choosing only the most polished, representative or surprising pieces.

The guiding editorial principle in selecting unpublished poems was quality and completeness. Ultimately, I rejected unpublished work that is decidedly fragmentary or unfinished. Alas, this meant the exclusion of many fascinating pieces that survive only in preliminary drafts, which anyway tend to be, as Peterson puts it, 'messy, chaotic, and difficult to read and identify'.[22] One such poem is a wartime tribute to Winston Churchill that begins 'Thou art a bulldog of true British breed' and ends 'And second only to our Gracious king.'[23] Another is 'The Abode of Love', a dramatic monologue uttered by an elderly woman recalling her Victorian childhood in a wealthy family who were members of the Agapemonite Church and were being courted by its founder, Henry Prince, for their money.[24] A third I regretted relinquishing is 'Highgate 1914', an account of schoolyard bullying later retold in 'Original Sin on the Sussex Coast' and *Summoned by Bells*.[25] One exception to the rule of rejecting poems in preliminary draft form is 'October Bells', which I was able to construct into a final state. In general, the editorial principle of quality and completeness meant that the likeliest contenders were poems sufficiently developed to make it into typescripts; however, a number of poems that survive only in holograph manuscript proved to be thoroughly developed and polished, and they therefore warranted consideration as well. Moreover, not all the poems in typescript that I uncovered merited publication: some were simply too thin, undeveloped or abstract. Ultimately, the decision to exclude had less to do with whether the poem was typed or handwritten; the quality and character of the poem drove the decision.

A secondary consideration was context. In general, I rejected poems ephemeral in nature, where the context seemed more significant than the poem itself, as well as poems written for purely personal or private purpose, many of which already appear in Bevis Hillier's three-volume biography of Betjeman or Candida Lycett Green's two-volume edition of her father's letters. A typical instance of an ephemeral exclusion is the poem Betjeman inscribed in Lennox Berkeley's copy of his *Collected Poems*, which begins:

'Twas in the Conservatorium
 That Freda and Lennox met
And through love of Art they became a part
 Of the famous Paddington Set.[26]

Although a lovely bit of light verse, its personal intention precludes it from *Harvest Bells*. Nevertheless, in the interest of presenting a truly surprising or unique perspective of Betjeman's mind or personality, I included some pieces that might otherwise have been deemed ephemeral – such for instance is 'A Squib on Norman Cameron', a hilarious if somewhat bawdy personal satire written in the vein of Alexander Pope. In this instance I felt its clever and unusual nature trumped my editorial principle of excluding personal ephemera.

An additional complication is presented by Betjeman's handwriting, which was notoriously illegible, as he confessed to Charles Abbott when sending him the first two manuscripts for the University of Buffalo's Poetry Collection: 'If I do not commit what I have written to the typewriter pretty well at once, I forget what I have written as I cannot read my own writing – nor will you be able to.'[27] Not long after this, Jock Murray wrote to Betjeman to respond to some suggestions about the production of *Old Lights for New Chancels*: 'We will do what we can about the paper. Your handwriting at that stage of your letter was not easily decipherable; but there was a word which we have taken to be "creamy". I hope this is right.'[28] Ultimately, if I found it problematic to decipher handwriting, it was usually an indication that the poem was in too preliminary a stage to warrant inclusion. Unfortunately, Betjeman's handwriting grew even worse with age and the onset of Parkinson's Disease, which precluded consideration of some very interesting late poems on environmental themes, including one that begins 'They have gone, those elms, that meant so much in our landskip', and another that begins 'Those hideous blocks that slam the sky'.[29] Their illegibility makes it impossible to determine whether they are complete. Another interesting piece lost to illegibility is 'Archie's Bells', a late poem reflecting on the haunting peals of Cornish church bells and written from the perspective of his old teddy bear Archie.[30]

A final editorial complication concerns punctuation and capitalization, particularly but not exclusively with the handwritten poems. The principle I followed in this matter is that of his original editors. Betjeman was careless and inconsistent with punctuation, illustrating the principle to Charles Abbott: 'I don't punctuate much you will see. I leave that to the publishers.'[31] Because he was vague about these matters, his work was regularly subjected to significant editorial intervention. I too have found this necessary upon occasion, silently inserting or altering punctuation when necessary to clarify the sense and syntax. This has been essential not only with those poems that survive in manuscript but even at times with published pieces.

In selecting previously published but uncollected poems for *Harvest Bells*, the decisions were surprisingly complicated. I began by considering the thirteen poems published in Betjeman's individual volumes that Lord Birkenhead excluded from *Collected Poems*. Of the twenty-one poems in *Mount Zion*, nine were rejected by Birkenhead when he edited the *Collected Poems*. I believe that he was correct to exclude 'A Seventeenth-Century Love Lyric', 'Mother and I', 'Tunbridge Wells', 'School Song', 'Arts and Crafts', and 'The Garden City'. They are trifles and nowhere near the standard that Betjeman set in 'Death in Leamington', which opens *Mount Zion*, and I too have excluded them. Any reader who wishes to read them can easily acquire a second-hand copy of *Mount Zion*, reissued in facsimile in 1975. However, Birkenhead was overly zealous in excluding 'St Aloysius Church, Oxford', 'Competition' and 'The Outer Suburbs' (the latter two among thirteen of *Mount Zion*'s poems reprinted in Betjeman's second collection, *Continual Dew*). I have included these three poems in this volume as pieces that should be restored to the canon, in one instance resuscitating Betjeman's original title. Two other volumes, *Continual Dew* and *A*

Few Late Chrysanthemums, also suffered exclusions from *Collected Poems* at the hand of Birkenhead. 'Tea with the Poets', 'The Wykehamist at Home', 'Clay and Spirit' and 'The Weary Journalist' deserve to be restored to the canon and are therefore included in this edition.[32]

But what of other published poems, those printed in periodicals or published as contributions to other books? The principle I started with is that if a poem had been published it merited initial consideration for inclusion in *Harvest Bells*. In the end, I included a sampling of published juvenilia and university verse, all uncollected periodical poems that have been identified, and several posthumous pieces. However, I excluded a number of short pieces commissioned late in Betjeman's life and designed for public occasion, such as these brief lines that appeared in 1979 to commemorate the reconsecration of a church tower:

> With weighty tick and solemn tock
> The pendulum swings to and fro
> For all four faces of the clock
> In your strange tower, St Anne's, Soho.[33]

I rejected similar ephemera, including book dedications, tributes to friends, conservation appeals, most of his laureate verse, and poetic captions for illustrations, particularly where the illustration was essential to appreciating the poem. Such items belong in a complete, scholarly edition of Betjeman's poetry, but their place is not in this collection. The reader is sure to find several exceptions, however, and here again I will plead the interest of presenting a truly surprising or unusual perspective on Betjeman's mind or personality.

I have attempted to arrange the poems in this collection chronologically by date of composition, though some of them cannot be dated conclusively, or (for the uncollected) by date of initial publication. Following the poems is a section of notes with commentary on individual poems, with such information as I have been able to unearth on each poem's origin and composition, contextual explanations of difficult allusions, and justification of any significant editorial intervention. The notes also state whether each piece is a newly discovered unpublished poem, or an uncollected poem previously printed in a newspaper, magazine, broadside or book but never added to the *Collected Poems*. If the poem was previously unpublished, I provide information on the manuscript(s) I consulted, though the reader is directed to Peterson's *John Betjeman: A Bibliography* for full details on the extant manuscripts and their variant states. I have also included two appendices. The first consists of a surprising and little-known translation Betjeman made of a Portuguese poem, in its several stages of development. The second contains a satirical poem previously attributed to another author, but for which I believe there to be significant evidence of Betjeman's possible authorship.

Several documented Betjeman poems have eluded my frustrated attempts to resurrect them. Bevis Hillier references two poems I have been unable to track down. In 1953, Murray and Betjeman were debating the contents for the upcoming publication of *A Few Late Chrysanthemums*. Hillier notes that 'The French poems were also axed' and then quotes a letter from Murray to Betjeman: 'I have read "Sacerdos in Aeternum" again and while still in part moved by it, doubts creep in. Its slightly dated flavour gives for some strange reason a hint of "The Young Reciter" and I think that this would become more pronounced in the cold light of print.' The mysterious poems in French were catalogued by Peterson as 'Deux Vieux Poésies Françaises' in the John Murray Archives, but they have since disappeared. No record of the priestly poem that reminded Murray of a musical revue has yet surfaced, though Hillier noted that 'The poem was rejected.'[34] Both represent instances of a great loss resulting from Betjeman's preferences being trumped by others. Another intriguing but missing poem is one entitled 'Lines Written on Learning of the Death of Earl Mountbatten of Burma'; Peterson records it as published in the *Daily Telegraph* on 28 September 1979.[35] After failing to find the poem in digital editions of the *Daily Telegraph*, and after unsuccessful queries at the newspaper's archives and the British Library's Newspaper Archive, I contacted Peterson, who unfortunately could not locate a copy but strongly recalled spotting it online. Until it turns up, he suggests, with his bibliographer's modest sense of humour, that it be classified as a 'Peterson ghost'.[36]

This volume of Betjeman's unpublished and uncollected poetry has gone to press with my awareness of gaps and a sense of irony that tomorrow a new Betjeman poem is likely to appear. Such was my fate ten years ago, when I compiled and edited Betjeman's *Poems in the Porch*, his poems about Church of England parish life that he read on radio in the 1950s. Within a year or two, a missing 'Poem in the Porch' appeared, one I had despaired of ever finding. It had been hiding from me in the University of Victoria's massive Betjeman collection.[37] Who knows what treasures are yet to be pulled from its depths? Thus I have resisted the urge to title this collection *Last Words*, a title Betjeman had proposed for the book that became *A Nip in the Air*. Instead, *Harvest Bells* is appropriated from the title of my favourite poem in this collection; it reminds us that poetry is food for the soul, and that it echoes across the ages even when the pen has ceased its scratching across the page.

NOTES

1   Betjeman's ten individual collections are *Mount Zion* (1931), *Continual Dew* (1937), *Old Lights for New Chancels* (1940), *New Bats in Old Belfries* (1945), *Selected Poems* (1948), *A Few Late Chrysanthemums* (1954), *Poems in the Porch* (1956), *High and Low* (1966), *A Nip in the Air* (1974) and *Uncollected Poems* (1982). *Collected Poems* (1958) went through multiple editions, eventually incorporating most of the contents of the ten individual volumes.

2   Cf. William S. Peterson, *John Betjeman: A Bibliography* (Oxford: Clarendon, 2006), pp. 48, 73, 132; Bevis Hillier, *John Betjeman: New Fame, New Love* (London: John Murray, 2002), pp. 187, 328, 392, 602.

3   Peterson, *John Betjeman*, pp. 132, 153, 170; Hillier, *Betjeman: The Bonus of Laughter* (London: John Murray, 2004), pp. 236, 385, 526–7.

4   Qtd. Hillier, *New Fame*, p. 393.

5   Peterson, *John Betjeman*, p. 97.

6   Letter from Jock Murray to Betjeman, 24 March 1955. Qtd. Peterson, *John Betjeman*, p. 97.

7   Hillier, *Bonus*, p. 527.

8   Letter to Charles D. Abbott, 10 March 1938. The Poetry Collection, The State University of New York at Buffalo, MS B520F4. An edited version of this letter is printed in Candida Lycett Green's collection (John Betjeman, *Letters, Volume One: 1926–1951* [London: Methuen, 1994], pp. 206–7).

9   Hillier, *Bonus*, 236; cf. Peterson, *John Betjeman*, pp. 48, 153.

10 Letter to Jock Murray, 7 December 1965. Qtd. Peterson, *John Betjeman*, p. 132.

11   Peterson, *John Betjeman*, p. xiv.

12   Peterson, *John Betjeman*, p. xvi.

13   Charles D. Abbott, 'Introduction', *Poets at Work: Essays Based on the Modern Poetry Collection at the Lockwood Memorial Library, University of Buffalo* (New York: Harcourt, 1948), pp. 11–12.

14   Abbott, 'Introduction', p. 12.

15   Abbott, 'Introduction', pp. 12–24.

16   Letter to David Posner, 6 July 1960. The Poetry Collection, The State University of New York at Buffalo, MS B520F9.

17   Letter to Charles D. Abbott, 10 March 1938. The Poetry Collection, The State University of New York at Buffalo, MS B520F4.

18   Postcard to Charles D. Abbott, 12 March 1938. The Poetry Collection, The State University of New York at Buffalo, MS B520F5.

19   Of the various sets of manuscripts and typescripts I consulted for editing Betjeman's unpublished poetry in this volume, the vast majority came from two libraries, Buffalo (seventeen mss) and Victoria (nineteen mss); in addition, five mss came from Yale, two each from the John Murray Archives and the University of Texas, and one each from Leeds, Eton, the British Library, the New York Public Library and Christ Church Archives, Oxford.

20   Cf. Hillier, *New Fame*, p. 248.

21   Alan Bell, 'The Times Profile: Sir John Betjeman. By Appointment: Teddy Bear to the Nation', *The Times*, 20 September 1982, p. 5.

22   Peterson, *John Betjeman*, p. 388.

23   The Poetry Collection, The State University of New York at Buffalo, MS B43F11.

24   Betjeman Archive, the British Library, Add. MS 71936, fol. 180. This unfinished poem was probably inspired by Aubrey Menen's historical novel of the same title, which Betjeman reviewed in the *Daily Telegraph* on 1 March 1957, though he wrote about the Agapemonites at various times in his life.

25 Betjeman Archive, the British Library, Add. MS 71645, fol. 66. Multiple drafts of this poem exist, all in six-line stanzas of rhyming iambic pentameters.

26 John Murray Archives.

27 Letter to Charles D. Abbott, 10 March 1938. The Poetry Collection, The State University of New York at Buffalo, MS B520F4. In editing this letter for publication, Candida Lycett Green made an understandable but nonetheless felicitous error in substituting 'God' for 'you': 'nor will God be able to' (*Letters, Volume One: 1926–1951*, p. 206).

28 Letter from Jock Murray to John Betjeman, 20 November 1939. The Poetry Collection, The State University of New York at Buffalo, MS B43F8.

29 Brotherton Library, University of Leeds, Elliott Collection MS Betjeman/3. These manuscripts were purchased at auction by the Brotherton Library in 2005 and were formerly in the possession of bookseller Reg Read, who met Betjeman in 1977 and served him from that point on as 'librarian, companion and court jester' (Hillier, *Bonus*, p. 499).

30 McPherson Library Special Collections, University of Victoria, John Betjeman Collection, MS PTO 002.

31 Letter to Charles D. Abbott, 10 March 1938. The Poetry Collection, The State University of New York at Buffalo, MS B520F4.

32 In compiling *Collected Poems*, Birkenhead's decisions may have owed as much to carelessness as to fastidiousness. Willy-nilly he changed some of the sequencing of poems, and when he decided to include 'The Heart of Thomas Hardy', which had never been published anywhere, even in periodical form, he inserted it in the section of poems from *Old Lights for New Chancels* rather than in a section of previously unpublished poems (which he grouped together under the limiting and unimaginative title 'Poems Written After 1954'). In fact, Betjeman had initially proposed it for inclusion in *Old Lights* but had second thoughts about its quality, so he and

Murray decided to reject it (cf. Hillier, *New Fame*, pp. 182–3; Peterson, *John Betjeman*, p. 417), and it was not published until Birkenhead included it in *Collected Poems*.

33   Published in the *Daily Telegraph*, 27 September 1979, to commemorate the newly restored tower of St Anne's Church, Soho.

34   Hillier, *New Fame*, pp. 488, 489; Peterson, *John Betjeman*, p. 406.

35   Peterson, *John Betjeman*, p. 432. This poem is also recorded in Peter Gammond and John Heald, *A Bibliographical Companion to Betjeman* (Guildford: The Betjeman Society, 1997), 79P6.

36   Correspondence with the author, 2 December 2008. Bevis Hillier also has no knowledge of this poem, not even its title (correspondence with the author, 26 July 2018).

37   It appeared too late to be included where it belongs, in *Poems in the Porch: The Radio Poems of John Betjeman* (London: Continuum, 2008). However, it appears in this collection under the title 'The Divine Society'.

HARVEST BELLS

NEW AND UNCOLLECTED POEMS
BY
JOHN BETJEMAN

A.D. 1980

The day was dark and overcast,
   The sun was shining bright;
But as it was behind a cloud
   It did not show its light.

But what care I for cloud or sun
   Or moon, or mist or rain;
The earth is lighted night and day
   By Osram's Neverwane.

The pre-historic chaps who lived
   In nineteen twenty-four
Thought they were very wonderful
   With wireless to the fore.

But now, in nineteen eighty, we
   Have made enormous strides;
We fly with Smith's Electroscope
   And eat 'Pill-food' besides;

And if we want to go to Mars
   We board an Aerosaur
Which, better than those aeroplanes,
   Takes you from door to door.

So drink to nineteen eighty, come
   Imbibe it with a will,
For scientists have not yet made
   Our drinks into a pill.

YE OLDE COTTAGE (QUITE NEAR A TOWN)

The happy haunt of typists common, pert.
   'We're in the country now!' they say, and wear
   Tweed clothes, and let the wind disturb their hair,
And carry ash sticks. 'Don't be silly, Gert!
Afraid of cows?' 'Oh Elsie, mind my skirt,
   It will get muddy.' 'Oh just look! down there
   A factory. . . .' 'Oh dearest, how they dare
To ruin all the country with their dirt!'

And Gert and Elsie's cottage – 'just too sweet'
   With rustic furniture, no bath, no drains,
     But still it is *so* countrified. A friend
Can sleep upon the sofa. And they eat
   Off pottery (hand-painted). Oh! the pains
     And saving for their game of let's pretend!

THE SONG OF A COLD WIND

The song of the wind in the telegraph wires,
  The breathing wind of the downs,
The wind that whistles through twenty shires
  Of red-roofed country towns.

'By river-water splashing
  I whirl the creaking mills,
As their great flat sails come crashing,
  I fly . . . and my laughter shrills
Up to the reach at Horning,
  Over the windy Bure,
As I leap from the arms of the morning,
  Fresh and bitter and pure.

'I batter a Cambridge village,
  And the copses, straight and dry,
Through bleak, brown stretches of tillage
  I run to a rainy sky.
Close Oxford lanes are muddy
  With elm leaves trampled brown,
So I worry a scholar at study,
  Or swallow one up in his gown.

'I swing on a Berkshire steeple;
  Below in the transept dim
I freeze the parson and people,
  And lose the place in the hymn.
To the rolling downland after
  I quicken. My whole self stirs

And I vent my life in laughter
   On the lonely clumps of firs.

'Somerset bells are tolling
   To warn rough Devon of me,
Where her red-patched hills are rolling
   Severn-ward and to sea.
But my Cornish soul arouses,
   And gathers its rushing wrath,
And I blow the slates from the houses
   Onto the garden path.

'In low grey cottages, clinging
   In mist round lichened spires,
They hear me sighing and singing
   And pile the peat on the fires.
I rush down wry roads frantic
   Where boats in harbour lie,
And I fling me on the Atlantic
   And drive it up to the sky.'

The song of the wind in the telegraph wires,
   The breathing wind of the downs,
The wind that whistles through twenty shires
   Of red-roofed country towns.

A SENTIMENTAL POEM

For the last time the light on the tamarisk bushes
    Swinging and swaying with glittering drops of rain;
For the last time the wrinkled ferryman pushes
    From Padstow quay again.

For the last time that sound of eternal wonder
    The crash of the wave and the hiss of the surf up the
      sand;
The silence before the next one breaks in thunder
    Shaking the feet of land.

For the last time the sound of an east wind singing,
    Among the spiked grey grasses, its pisky tunes,
And the feel of the dry sand, face and bare knees stinging,
    As it whirls along the dunes.

For the last time in green pools, still and eerie,
    Low tides reveal the tresses of mermaids' hair
Caught in old spars and anchors, and murmurs, weary,
    On white sands hard and bare.

For the last time – but the stone-hedged lane is winding
    And long it takes to climb to the top of the hill
Whence we will look, tho' the silver tears be blinding,
    On old friend Ocean still.

SWEETS AND CAKE

Neville stodged with sweets and cake
Lay by the pavvy half awake,
And as he lay he felt the squeeze
Of something hard above his knees.
And near him sprawling on the grass
He saw the sturdy little arse
Of Teddy Sale. 'Oh, Teddy dear,
Stop chewing grass; roll over here.'
Two light blue eyes, a freckled face,
An open shirt, the supple grace
Of young and well-advanced fifteen
Crawled over to him through the green.
'I say, you're awfully decent, Ted.
Let's find a place and go to bed.'
With arms around each other tight,
They found a resting-place all right.
And soon as they were settled in,
Neville whispered, 'Let's begin.
Come on, here's mine . . . let's look at yours.'
Ted leapt upon him on all fours
And pressed his trousers on the face
Of his companion for a space.
Neville gasping hard for air
Undid the flies and felt some hair
And, hard and warm, another toy –
The tool of his beloved boy.
'Look out, I'm coming!' Teddy cries,
And further he undoes his flies,

And up and down he rubs his prick.
'Kiss me, Neville, kiss me quick!'
He kissed . . . he gulped the semen fast,
And when the ecstasy was passed
They both got up. 'How *could* you squirt
That nasty stuff all down my shirt!'

DENTIST'S DINING ROOM

The Throwley Forstal Dental Surgeon
   Likes mahogany chairs,
And a tall red sideboard
   With mirrors in rounds and squares.

He likes to see the cruet stand,
   Bright in the setting sun,
From the big bow window
   When the dental day is done.

He likes to know that his wifie
   Is cooking up Irish stew,
And the Drage-Way table
   Looks like new.

So he likes to pour his Guinness
   Himself, because of the froth,
For he likes the tone of
   Having no tablecloth.

The black cat calendar hangs
   White on the orange and black,
'Wifie's Birthday
   And dentistry rather slack'.

But he clutches the stencilled gift book
   With loops of leatherwork hung –
A ninety-eighth edition of
   When We Were Very Young.

'Take her along to the pictures
   Out of the Tudor hall,
Over the crazy paving,
   Sorry to leave it all.'

SEZINCOTE

If those domes could only speak,
    If those turnip tops could talk,
If those wonderfully life-like Nandi bulls
    Could rise on their legs and walk;

If those prickles and spikes and carvings
    Could climb from each golden wall
And march in a phalanx of stone and lead
    Into the entrance hall;

If the tinted glass in the dairy
    And the god from the temple pond
Could join with the palm tree shaded
    By its Coade and Seely frond;

If the mermaid out in the garden
    Could put down her basin and dress,
If the moss-covered snakes in the fountain
    Gave utterance more or less;

If the beautiful Wellington chimney
    Could join the procession today,
And all were assembled under the dome,
    What do you think they'd say?

What would they say to the Colonel
    As they crowded the graceful stairs
And overflowed in the ballroom
    And sat on the Empire chairs?

What would they say to the Colonel
  With their throats of crumbling stone
(Cotswold or Coade and Seely)
  In a sad unanimous groan?

They would say, 'God bless you, dear Colonel,
  And Butler and Leslie and Green,
For neatly repairing the Orangery.
  We remember what it has been.

'Sir Charles was devoted to it,
  And so was the Lady Anne.
It served as a run for their lap dogs
  As only an Orangery can.

'The smile of the Indian lotus,
  The scent of the jasmine rare,
Delighted the various Rushouts
  Who sat out the dances there.

'When starlight shone on the stonework
  Out of the Cotswold sky,
They admired that crescent of Indian art
  As the English clouds went by.

'They watched the shimmering moonlight
  Shine on the Orangery dome.
Oh Colonel, do please restore it,
  And we'll all go happily home.'

PASTORAL INCIDENT

Down where the Irish heifers start and thud
Along towards one as they chew the cud,
Bold walked the Colonel brandishing his spud.
Not far away – a few grey fields between –
In trailing gowns came Sezincotia's queen.
Humbly the brambles shivered and drew back
While rounded oaks lent shadows to her track,
When swift she lifted 'mid protesting cries
A yellow insect with enormous eyes.
Hark how it barks and how the heifers roar,
See now the Colonel, thinking of the war,
Holds back the brutes to let the lady pass,
Trailing her crepe-de-chine across the grass.
Let the *New Statesman* and the foul *Express*
Trumpet some public act of fearlessness;
But where those Cotswold Indian fountains play
Brave deeds are done, yea sev'ral times a day.

A SQUIB ON NORMAN CAMERON

Now let my muse to puff'd up CAM'RON stray
And hide her candle in his blinding Day.
Was e'er there seen such concentrated Pride,
Such slobb'ring Lechery and Pomp beside?
Was e'er there seen (Impatience be thou still)
A slower climber up Parnassus' hill?
O bloody C-M-R-N! How I hate thy soul!
And to thy *face* I consecrate my *hole.*

BLISLAND, BODMIN

The moorland parish has thin elms,
Tall spinsters of the village green,
And slate by stone wet houses stand
Where dwellings must have always been.

The church lies low upon the hill,
And thick and strong is raised her tower
Of hardest surface granite stones,
Stuffed in between with fern and flower

On west side only; darker grey
The east and north, more soaked with rain,
String course and moulding washed away
Beneath the metal weather-vane.

We threaded headstones; in the church,
The late rough granite bays between,
We saw the ribbed old plaster roof
Cut under by a chancel screen.

Silent a valley stream outside,
The birds and growing plants were still.
We almost heard the golden light
Fall on low arches from the hill.

First love and life, that April day
Stood open at a moorland shrine:
And beauty, fading, only made
My thoughts all his and his thoughts mine.

Scatter bells and shatter night!
You burst about a foreign land!
The sullen church, the lonely stars
Shall fright not yet my guiding hand.

HOME THOUGHTS FROM EXILE

When I picture the scenes of my prime
    In a little North Hinksey abode,
I can fancy the warm summer-time
    Still breathes o'er Divinity Road:
I can hear Holy Trinity bells
    That entranced me in Gasworks Lane
Where I swotted in spite of the gas and the smells
    From a pungent and neighbourly drain.

I remember the jolly suppers,
    The swipes and the kippers and all.
I remember my first year's cuppers;
    I'd have died for St Ernest's Hall.
I remember the boats like coffins
    When we rowed St Stephen's and won,
And I think of those gorgeous spreads in Boffin's
    Whenever I look at a bun.

I remember the chaps all thought me
    A bit of a corker then,
For Ethel and Gladys caught me
    (They were always dead nuts on men);
And next I was keen on Gertie
    (Gee! what a stunner for looks),
But she went and treated me downright dirty
    Though I gave her my old Mods books.

Ah, those were the days, you fellows,
    But the torch shall not fail nor fall,

While a man among you bellows
  'It's ho, for St Ernest's Hall!'
So keep the old flag flying
  And rally around the call
That cried and cries and will keep on crying,
  'Ho, for St Ernest's Hall!'

CHORUS

'Ho, for St Ernest's Hall!
It's ho, for St Ernest's Hall!
And it's ho, and it's ho, and it's ho, and it's ho,
And it's ho, for St Ernest's Hall!'

WORK

'Oh! have you any napkin rings,
  Hand-painted, gold and blue?
Or little stands for menu-cards?
  Or anything will do . . .

'Oh! stitch me up a leather gift,
  Or weave a raffia mat,
Or do me some batik-work,
  I'll wear a scarf of that.

'Oh! I've bought a gift for Elsie
  And I've bought a gift for Su:
And I've bought a lovely leather gift
  At Liberty's for you.'

POPULAR SONG

'Oh, what are you doing down Harringay way?'
'Well, I bought a bit of ribbon in the Bon Marché –
    Crouch End, Stroud Green, you're calling to me,
    Home for supper or a hot high tea,
    Which, Aunt Ena, which shall it be?'

'Oh! Serviettes and Soviets don't mean so much to me
But I'm always all a-doodah when it come to cups of tea,
So let's share a pot per person in an A.B.C.
    Crouch End, Stroud Green, you're calling to me,
    Home for supper or a hot high tea,
    Oh, we'll share a pot per person in an A.B.C.'

NINE O'CLOCK

Now is the time when sturdy boys
    Do turn their bottoms to the sun
To scrub the entrances of shops
    And slop the water over one.

Now Edgar Speed and Mrs Bate
    Awakened from their bed of sin
Totter across their modern room
    To let the Bloomsbury morning in.

In the Hotel Great Central now
    In glazed and terracotta gloom
Lies Ernest Gladstone Alfred Parkes
    Left over in the Wharncliffe Room.

For Mac has gone to Osterley,
    Roberts to Bushey, Stein to Pinner.
He rests alone the last to leave
    From Marks and Spencer's Annual Dinner.

EMILY WREN

Higgledy-piggledy Emily Wren
Wheels her tricycle out again.
'Chariot', 'Singer', or plain 'Sunbeam'?
What does it matter, it goes like a dream.

Higgledy-piggledy Emily Wren
Wheels her tricycle out again.
She goes to purchase Hubby and Flo
Presents for Xmas, but they don't know
What her string bag will have inside
When she returns from her tricycle ride.

One, two, what about Sue,
Next year's calendar ought to do;
Three, four, that old bore –
A handkerchief-sachet for Ma-in-law.
Five, six – the pedal sticks –
A cruet-stand or candlesticks.
Seven, eight, for Auntie Kate,
Her birthday comes so very late.
Nine, ten, a good fat hen
For Xmas dinner, thought Emily Wren.

Higgledy-piggledy down the road
Past Mrs Morris' new abode,
Over the tram-lines, through the square,
Park St, Bridge St, Austin and Ware,
Now freewheeling, oh, what a spree!
If only Aunt Katie or Hubby could see.

Eleven, twelve, oh, the yells!
Thirteen, fourteen, horses snorting,
Fifteen, sixteen, stamping, kicking,
Seventeen, eighteen, framework breaking,
Nineteen, twenty, there are plenty
Hearses driven to the cem'try.

Higgledy-piggledy Emily Wren
Never will go to the town again,
Never again a tricycle ride
For the trike is scrap metal along the roadside.

Higgledy-piggledy that is the end,
For the tricycle proved a recalcitrant friend.

THE TAMARISKS

The tamarisks parading on the shore,
Leaves that recall the dreary immortelle,
Are conscious now that something was before
And will be after their perennial spell
Of uneventful bloom, unmitigated gloom;
For tamarisks will flourish when the sun
Has burnt itself to cinders: even so their bloom
Must not be spared the final hecatomb
Wherein the records of our passions perish
The hideous scroll of sentiments we cherish.
The tamarisks, the English bourgeoisie,
Batten upon the bloom they procreate,
Fatten upon the gloom they generate,
The uneventful bloom, unmitigated gloom,
The lasting victims to their ravenous womb.
But when the day of reckoning cometh they,
Wilting upon the cinders of the sun,
Will move their dreary arms to stay
The scimitar no tamarisk can shun;
The tamarisks, the dreary bourgeoisie,
That have outlived their own eternity,
Falling at last for lack of husbandry.

SONNET

The silent ghosts of morning, where are they?
　Not yet their fingers wander from the East
　To tap my casements, draw aside the creased
And tattered curtains from my sleepless lay,
Nor stir to scatter all these glooms away.
　But from the watch-tower of my thoughts at least
　There springs the promise of the slow dawn's feast
For eyes weary of waiting for the day,

Wherewith the dewy hopes will not be long
　Coming to crown the wakeful palimpsest
With glories and the attributes of song.
　　The black hours and the vigil linger yet,
　As though some Sleep-God's wrong can be redressed
　　Only by slow enforcement of regret.

WISTERIA BRANCHES

The lank wisteria branches of my mind
Droop into slow sad ecstasies.
They drink the uttermost perfume of my being,
The inebriate being of my perfume undefined.

In consequence these sad wisteria branches
Muse singly, and their gentle rhythm
Is but the trembling of a mind bereft,
Whose sympathies and solaces have left
That the last drained petal marble-cold slowly, palely
    blanches.

A POEM BY MY OLD BEAR ARCHIBALD

No bear however bat-like in appearance,
  No bear however bear-like 'neath the moon,
Can quite forget the sudden, smart uprearance
  Of Mr Gladstone in a spun cocoon.

No porcelain arch nor congregated ruin,
  No distant prospect when the day is done,
No antique grot which antique bears can coo in
  Is that cocoon which Mr Gladstone spun.

Forever and forever and forever
  No killing bottle, chrysalis or spoon,
Only the vain winds that cry out 'Endeavour!'
  And Mr Gladstone in his spun cocoon.

HARVEST BELLS

How loud from Bourton-on-the Hill
    Ring out the Harvest bells!
How can their climbing music still
    What country silence tells!

The elms have got the ivy round,
    The little bridge is crumbling,
And how insistent is the sound
    Of weedy water tumbling.

And there among the dying things
    Where Cotswold stone is falling,
Alert and struggling with their wings
    The furtive ants are crawling;

Plant, animal and insect kills –
    From here to Temple Guiting,
The earth is swollen up with hills
    From ages of their fighting.

A bedpost on an upper floor,
    A wheezy, muffled crying,
Upstairs behind the wooden door
    A seventh child is dying.

Too full! Too full! The Bourton chimes
    Of harvesting and gleaning;
They stutter like the headstone rhymes
    And tremble with their meaning.

COUNTRY SILENCE

Country noises do not shake
The surface of the silent lake.
The silent lake through which I see
Is life and death at rest in me.
Country noises have no power
In this diversity of flower.
Drop by drop the horse hoofs fall
Outside the sunny garden wall.
For all their sound of summer seas
Still green and crested rise the trees,
Till the collected sound has made
A brave and miniature cascade –
The hop and scratching of the thrush,
The bees about the currant bush,
The crackle of the garden fire,
The swooping of the chapel choir,
The barking dogs where children play,
And windows flung across the way,
And melancholy bells that make
A hidden current through the lake:
The silent lake through which I see
Is life and death at rest in me.

CHANNEL CROSSING

Let us, you and I, meander
To the shore where bold Leander
Stripped and struck his limbs of iron
Against the waves, or was it Byron?
Both, I guess. The one was driven
By an impulse seldom given
To our moderns, logic-riven;
But the other's proud translation
Was poetic emulation.
    In these famed aquatic flights,
    Both have been eclipsed by Gleitze.

EIGHTEENTH-CENTURY PRINT

A canal, brown water
sluicing through some broken boards, the daughter
of the lock-keeper repairing them, and hindered
by their sad proximity to what
was once a Roman bridge, Cotswold stone and timbered,
over which a mossed and cobbled track
leads a tired peasant on a piebald hack
laboriously surmounting it: whereon a stack
round and misshapen patiently suggests
a chapel of Saint Mary Magdalen
perched as a corbel long deprived of Seraphim,
lax invitation where the pilgrim with his conscience rests.
Behind, Lechlade's mature derogatory spire
points to the fleece that bleaches the marine
welkin as though it dared conspire
against the landskip placid and serene:
but this mute chastisement is lost
on my brown horseman now the lode is safely crossed,
the cobbles smitten by the rare footfall,
their worn millennium shaken by the close relation
of slow repressed rusticity
(it is not hard to find a parallel
between the obdurate rustic and his own material),
the chapel scarcely heeded in the arduous translation,
and Saint Mary left to wonder at the latest generation.

LERICI 1930

Farflung, I
Tamper not with pleasure but decry
Its gestures and pursue them not
Whether they be all terrestrial or celestial.

Rarely too
It answers to the call; I conjure you
To harvest grape and bergamot
And lose your reason hoping for the fruitful season.

I have set
My music to the sound of clarinet
And tamed my spirit to attune
With its bland wooing, unrewarded for my doing.

Now at least
My own reflections are the ample feast,
And they come seldom quite immune
From preconception, free from the hope of their reception.

EVANGELICAL HYMN

Hear my prayer, divine Redeemer,
 As my heart for beauty pants.
To the poet, to the dreamer
 Grant sufficient for his wants.

Blest divine beknown Redeemer
 At thy feet I take my stand,
Where thine oriflammic streamer
 Wraps about fair Albion's land.

Now unto the great Redeemer
 Vesper bells the rustics call,
From the plotter and the schemer
 Planning ruin for men all.

From hell's torments, blest Redeemer,
 Let thine own redemption bring,
A fit offering men would deem a
 Worthy gift from such a king.

SUDDEN CONVERSION

Burn down the embers
   And turn down the light,
I will not be wanting
   Wincarnis tonight.
No wine, no nor spirits
   Can help since I heard
From the minister's lips
   The acceptable word.
The gaslight in Bethel
   To me is more dear
Than the radiant rays
   From my electrolier.
Go, Moll, get my handbag,
   Come, Doll, to my side:
I've altered my will
   And the Lord will provide.

ZION

The Independent Calvinistic
   Methodist Chapel is gone;
Dust in the galleries, dust on the stairs,
   There was no one to carry it on;
And a Norman New Jerusalem Church
   Was raised on the sacred site,
Where they praised the Lord and praised the Lord
   By incandescent light.

The Gothic is bursting over the way
   With Evangelical song,
For the pinnacled Wesley Memorial Church
   Is over an hundred strong.
So what is a New Jerusalem
   Gas-lit and yellow-walled,
To that semicircular pitch-pine sea
   With electric light installed?

Crack your walls, Wesley Memorial!
   Shine bright, you electrolier!
Your traceried windows may split with song,
   New Jerusalem fall with fear;
Too brief, too brief any earthly fame,
   Hymns of the world declare;
See, see the Particular Baptist Church,
   For they've central heating there.

THE OUTER SUBURBS

The weary walk from Oakleigh Park
Through the soft suburban dark
Bedizened with electric lights
Which stream across these northern heights.
In blackened blocks against the view
Stands gabled Rosslyn Avenue,
And bright within each kitchenette
The things for morning tea are set.
A stained-glass window, red and green,
Shines, hiding what should not be seen,
While wifie knits through hubbie's gloom
Safe in the Drage-way drawing-room.
Oh, how expectant for the bed,
All 'Jacobethan' overhead!

ST ALOYSIUS CHURCH, OXFORD

Mary Mother, with what art
Worship we the Sacred Heart!
In what paint, what glass, what plaster
Stands the many-coloured master!

Aloysius, rich and poor
Must enter by Thy grained oak door
To realise with unreal eyes
Reality and paradise.

CHARTERHOUSE SCHOOL SONG

There's many an Old Carthusian
　　In the Café Royal now
Who likes the tar, the soldier and
　　The boy who drives the plough.

Floreat Carthusia!
　　Gaudeamus! Joy!
On sea or in the barrack,
　　Thank God I'm still the boy.

Yes, I'm an Old Carthusian,
　　And I'm a cup of tea,
But Sherborne, surely Sherborne
　　Was the proper school for me.

LONDON SPREADING

Those trees in awkward silence wait
A new 'Desirable Estate'.
In lines and scaffolding and tin
They contemplate the growth of sin.
And yet the very sin creates
Strange beauty from its new Estates.
Hard and red their houses frown
On where below lies Camden Town.
They cannot hear the coalmen call
Against each echoing stucco wall.
The terrace closed and tall and stark
Ignores the vulgar shout and bark,
But turns its blind back-garden eye
To where the laden barges lie
Upon the silent waterway.
'Ol' bottles, any rags today?'
Who knows what these dumb buildings feel
To watch their stucco peel and peel?

I. *In an Oxford Lodging*

She sat in the cosy parlour at tea
And looked at the child she had lately born
As though in its face, by care unworn,
She could trace her own inconstancy.
'Oh yes, Mrs Provost,' she said with a smile,
'My husband adores him. Perhaps in a while
He too will a little Recessionist be.'

And the rattle and chink of the front-door chain
That announced her husband's in-coming was heard.
'And how is our son?' said a voice from the hall,
'My darling – ' and there before the twain
Stood the Provost himself: nor could lip one word
At this awkward quandary for them all.

II. *At Tea*

'So you've brought him to tea,' she fawns with a smile.
    'How fine he will look when he gets a bit bigger.
'And another one coming?' She regards the while
    Her visitor's whalebone corseted figure.

And the rain outside gives an ominous tap
    At the dingy pane, and the gas lamps shine
On his curly head, and the whalebones snap
    As she bends to him thinking, 'If he were mine.'

But the child she bore lies screwed in a box,
    And she sees it again in its own short stay,
Living namelessly, as one who unlocks
    A cupboard forgotten until today.

THE HEARTLESS HEART'S EASE:
A LAMENT BY TOM MOORE

The calm of Combe Bisset is tranquil and deep
Where Ebble flows soft mid her downland asleep,
And there when the shadows were lengthy and late
I would stand by the doctor's small white wooden gate.

Oh, long have I stood there, when gay blew the breeze
Through the square cottage garden and stirred the heart's
    ease,
But heart's ease to me came a-pushing a pram
In the shape of sweet Pansy Felitia Lamb.

When the sun shone in patches and clouds scudded low,
I would wait for the doctor to pack up and go,
With his camp stool and easel and brushes and paint,
To look for a view that was rural and quaint.

Ah, 'twas then I would enter and bide near the door
To list to my lady a-sweeping the floor,
And perhaps catch a sight of her, golden and mild,
As she stooped to caress her poor petulant child.

How I wished as I hid, those caresses were mine
And that she and the doctor would ask me to dine.
I would shew that e'en I was a highbrow as well
And I'd sing local songs with my voice like a bell.

Long I stood by the door and the weather grew cold,
And the heart's ease decayed and went back to the mould,
And the sleet beat their cottage and dark grew the sky,
And she and the doctor grew haughty and high.

I went to the church and I prayed to dear God
That they both would vouchsafe me a smile or a nod,
Or that I would get 'arty' and thus would get on
With the Guinnesses, Gertler and Sickert and John.

I neglected my ploughing and soon got the sack,
And I had no Colleen for to welcome me back,
For heartless was Pansy Felitia Lamb,
And it's sad and half-witted she thinks that I am.

Oh, the calm of Combe Bisset is tranquil and deep
Where Ebble flows soft mid her downland asleep.
Unemployed and unwanted I still stand and wait
For the heart's ease to blossom and smile by the gate.

THE MOST POPULAR GIRL IN THE SCHOOL

It isn't the same at St Winifred's now Monica's left the
    school.
She was so calm and collected, cultivated and cool.
I shall never forget the example she set to a girl like me
By the way she carried her rifle in St Winifred's O.T.C.

Oh, she was cunning at ball games, and I shall never
    forget
The way she managed at tennis – just to pop them over
    the net.
Her opponents didn't much like it and made a bit of a stir,
But of course it was all quite different, if *you* were playing
    with *her.*

She was excellent too at cricket, though her glasses were
    rather thick.
And she did her best in the field – but of course she wasn't
    too quick.
But her slowness told in her bowling and every one of us
    found
We were bowled by her cunning googlies – sort of – along
    the ground.

Gosh, I was fond of Monica – she was a regular sport.
It was rotten for her her complexion seemed to fall rather
    short
Of what is expected of schoolgirls – but I think it's a filthy
    disgrace
To say that a girl looks ugly just 'cos she's spots on her
    face.

Monica wasn't a beauty – but still she had plenty of grit,
And I'll give you all an example of how she showed heaps
    of it.
We had water sports on at the swimming baths, and
    when we were going to begin,
Someone pushed at the back, and because of it the
    Geography mistress fell in.

Well, Monica hated the water, but she hit on a brilliant
    scheme.
She did what she could on the edge then – for she was the
    first to scream.
We hauled our Geography mistress safe out and sound as
    a bell,
But some of us mightn't have noticed, had it not been for
    Monica's yell.

No, it isn't the same at St Winifred's, now Monica's left
    the ranks,
So we've all saved up to give her a farewell token of
    thanks:
The yarn of a regular ripper – as sporty and straight as a
    rule
In a nice limp leather edition – 'The Most Popular Girl in
    the School'.

THE ELECTRIFICATION OF LAMBOURNE END

How ALBERT SPARKE has licences to sell
Both beer and spirits in his new Hotel:
How he, who once sold paltry pints of beer,
Now profits in Martini shall appear.
My muse shall show how small the changes are
Which make a palm court of a public bar:
How Albert's income rose from night to night
From fifty pounds to fifteen hundred quite
Largely because of *the Electric Light*.
    Far from a railway or a turnpike road,
Embowered in elm trees, stood 'The Tranter's Load',
A neat, square building, elegant not great
(On this side hawthorns and on that the gate).
It looked, when men return'd from making hay,
The jovial part that it was meant to play.
The squeaking hinge, worn bright by constant twirls,
Would warn the host of slow approaching churls.
With bar well sanded and a counter clear,
The beaming Albert sparkled like his beer.
Scoggins would come and Boggins Higgs would bring
And o'er their modest halves of bitter sing,
Till Albert jokingly would prod their calves
And say their wives were their more modest halves.
The lonely traveller, listening to the din
Beside the wicket, would be tempted in
And further fun and riot would begin.
And when the sunset, flattening on the hills,
Brought in its train a sullen evening's chills,
Then Albert shut the day's departing out

With two-barred shutters fastened in a grout.
And next, to brighten up the sons of toil,
He lit the lamps which kept alight through oil.
　　Say, did you see in yonder cupboard stored
A heavy, deeply-pitted, elmwood board?
And did you on its ancient surface trace
Enlarging circles round a central space?
This, once the solace of all rustic hearts,
Alas! now used no more, was used for darts.
And, reader, on the palm court ceiling look,
Do you not notice one belated hook?
From that, when Boggins, Higgs and Scoggins sung,
The old oil lamp would rattle as it hung.
　　How changed this once familiar rustic sight?
'Twas largely due to *the Electric Light*.
　　On June the seventh, nineteen twenty-four,
They made a bypass pass by Albert's door.
Boggins, when crossing to 'The Tranter's Load',
With slow, uneven pace athwart the road,
Ere yet the hinge could squeak his long'd approach,
Was killed by a 'Delight of Bourneville' coach.
And Higgs is leaving Lambourne End for Zion,
While Scoggins now goes over to 'The Lion'.
So people pass, customs and custom too.
And what, please Heav'n, is Albert Sparke to do?
　　The fifth of April, nineteen twenty-five,
Saw two tall pylons near the Inn arrive.
By June the seventeenth did Albert Sparke
Have more than just his name to light the dark:
Then see his swift prosperity begin
From 'Bass on draught' to 'Here's a good pull in!'
And thence to 'Teas and Good Accommodation'.

A pleasant outlook on the petrol station
Tempted the chauffeur; while, to please his master,
Black beams were painted on 'The Tranter's' plaster.
And in electric bulbs the tale was told:
'This house is over seven centuries old.'
What matter if 'twas six whole centuries out,
When Albert Sparke knew what he was about?
A floodlight on the front brought hundreds here,
And spirits rose while downward went the beer.
    See, how the new and mediæval porch
Is lighted by an imitation torch!
Meanwhile, within, what changes Albert made!
Each glowing bulb has its appointed shade –
A lantern this, and in the drawing-room
More modernistic notes dispel the gloom.
Now to 'The Tranter's Load' in crowds appear
Those whose delight is just to sit and leer.
With hair as shiny as their cars outside,
They chaff and riddle, chortle and deride.
Pleas'd to hold forth, with pleasure they defend
The rights of Woking, here in Lambourne End.
    Who is that man with Old Harrovian tie,
Enliven'd footwear and commercial eye?
That prosp'rous, gentlemanly business shark?
Why that, fond reader, that is Albert Sparke.
See what *Electric Light* with transport's aid
Has brought to him who understands his trade.
The signboard is repainted o'er the door:
Not 'Tranter's Load', but now 'La Nuit d'Amour'.

EDGWARE

Years ago the Duke of Chandos
    Lived in Canons Park at ease,
Rows of footmen fluttered round him
    If his grace but chanced to sneeze.
In a labour-saving dwelling
    Situated on the site,
Mrs Seascale in the bathroom
    Curls her hair on Friday night,
But the ducal ghost one evening
    Met her, so she murmured, 'Pardon,
Don't disturb my little Nellie
    Doing homework in the garden.'

'I knocked out my pipe on my old flannel bags,
    I lay back and thought about Kant.
Bees hummed the solicitor's garden in;
    I am empiric: bees aren't.

'I felt for my 'baccy jar up on a shelf
    With its New College Crest done in yellow.
Boys called in the Methodist Sunday School –
    I am a sociable fellow.

'I reached for my copies of *Hegel* and *Locke*,
    Longinus and *Plato*, although
Sun shone on the rectory tennis court,
    I am agnostic, you know.

'Jolly old Winchester! jolly old New College!
    Cream of our fine middle classes!
By cheerful unbendings in soccer and social clubs
    We can get on with the masses.'

TEA WITH THE POETS

Three pink Hampstead intellectuals,
 Three thin *passé* Bloomsbury dons
Sit discussing Manley Hopkins
 Over Mr Grogley's dainty scones.

Three great hunks of bread and butter,
 Three great lumps of Cheddar cheese,
Big legs sprawling in the roadway
 Friends of Stephen Spender lie at ease.

Tucking in at whipped cream walnuts,
 Blue shorts bursting under green,
C. Day Lewis brings his wolf cubs
 Safe into the full canteen.

But when the Major lets the net down,
 When I see that cotton dress,
When we move to the verandah,
 When I put my racket in its press –

Then comes the tea time of all I like best
With my long-leggéd, blubber-lipped,
 carefree, uncorsetted,
  fun-freckled
  PRIMULA GUEST.

A POET'S PRAYER

Killing time
Filling space
Undermine
The human race.

The hour gone
Shortens life
More surely than
The murderer's knife.

The idle word
Upon the pen
May degrade
The minds of men.

From wasted hour
And wanton word
With all your power
Keep me, Lord.

ON MISS E. BADGER, 9 BEVERLEY GARDENS, WEMBLEY PARK, MIDDLESEX, WHO SAT OPPOSITE TO ME ON THE GWR, ASCENSION DAY 1939

Why bother to smile and get sexy?
Much better a book of devotion –
So easy a body to capture,
Why does she wear grey flannel?
And that ridiculous scarf clip?
Who will they ever excite,
Based on the patterns in *Woman*?
And then, if I get the flesh,
The turbulent mouth and warm shoulder,
The shiny globular legs
Cased in ladderless stockings,
Then, if I get to know
What the lips are like when they open,
And come to dread the approach
Of evening, sitting and smoking
In our shiny upholstered
Bed-above bed-above parlour,
What are blue eyes but blue jelly?
The tilt of the nose but a cover
For two black holes in a skull face?
And what are thick thighs but thin thigh bones
Lying, in seventy years,
In the Garden of Rest at Stoke Poges?

BIG BUSINESS

Kind little clerks have been caught in the can
Of the great big-business fishing man.
'Yours on appro. at nothing per cent':
That's what the tastefully laid bait meant.
It looked high-class, good style, secure,
In the premier, art, deluxe brochure.
'Re. ours of the ult., we beg to state':
That was the hook in the handsome bait.
'We have not received your payment to hand
As per promise; please understand
Unless' – unless – UNLESS – **UNLESS**.
I didn't order it. I didn't guess.
I didn't know that he meant cash down.
I didn't care for the thing, I own.
But the wife – of course she was dazzled by
The gentleman's Old Harrovian tie.
I didn't know that he wouldn't wait.
Good-bye NW 78!
Good-bye 'St Elmo'! Good-bye front hall,
And my bedroom suites – he has hooked you all.
Dawn over Metroland. Swift and serene
Glides into Neasden the seven-fifteen.
He won't catch me with his damned plain van.
I'll die on the line and not in the can.

CHESTNUT HAIR

Spawn of the Rector's son on Polly Knapp.
   How did she get that shock of chestnut hair?
   It took her up to London, kept her there,
And shone down Praed Street, blinded many a chap.
Homing Great Westernwards, it caught him slap,
   Pulled up the taxi, quadrupled the fare,
   And lured him down the steps in Norfolk Square.
The basement door slammed after, like a trap.

A shilling for the metre, twenty more,
   The Good Luck Calendar, the smell of stew,
     The Dismal Desmond sprawling on the bed.
His eyes looked loving on the things she wore,
   On high-heeled shoes that Polly never knew,
     And drowned and drowned in waves of falling
       red.

Club, canteen, Victoria, Grand and Mauretania
Sinus, neurasthenia and of course depressive mania –
Local maladjustment and an overall collapse
Telephonic twitters and a home-brewed with the chaps:
Rather too much bonhomie and quite a lot of spite
Go to make a real routine and fill another night.
Club, canteen, Victoria, Mauretania, Grand,
Canteen, club, Victoria, the Mauretania and –
    'Hello, you from Manchester? How long are you
       down?'
    'Come for the duration. Well, what's it like, this
       town?'
    'Oh, fun. Let's have one at the Club, or here in the
       canteen.
    Of course it's bad, although we're not as busy as
       we've been.
    There's lots to do, and entre-nous we're rather
       under-manned
    Well chaps, the Mauretania? Victoria? Well, the
       Grand.'
And still he talked, and still the wonder grew
That one small head could carry that home-brew.

ORDER REIGNS IN WARSAW

Wide squares of Warsaw! Salty blows the north wind
Over standing water from the Baltic to Ukraine;
Bending miles of reed bed, beating hollow churches,
It whistles round the castles that are building on the plain.

Most serene republic! The model among nations,
This was the Poland where Copernicus was born,
White-painted cottages and many hands for harvest
Where peninsulas of pinewood are gulfed about in corn.

'Order reigns in Warsaw.' Only eighty years ago,
Empty streets . . . and houses, still as bolt and bar;
Bitterly the north wind set the bodies swinging,
Hanging up for Poland by the order of the Czar.

'Order reigns in Warsaw' . . . the splendid, newest order,
The order of the rifle shot and truncheon for the Pole,
Electrocuting wire, blasphemy and murder,
Beating out the body to liberate the soul.

Hard tonight the searchlights sweep the camps of Poland
And crowded open cattle trucks, the Pole beside the Jew
Dying in the ice cold, the tender arms of tyranny.
'Order reigns in Warsaw.' But is the order new?

Here now in Dublin are many-candled churches,
Living Irish people, kneeling in the glow.
THERE . . . where the snow falls thick on baroque altar
Lie those who served them, bodies in the snow.

Wide square of Warsaw! Salty blows the north wind
Over standing water from the Baltic to Ukraine.
Wide from the world come the fighting men of Poland,
Flying, sailing, marching till Poland rise again.

PROLOGUE SPECIALLY WRITTEN FOR THE 70TH ANNIVERSARY GAIETY THEATRE, DUBLIN

The strains of Balfe! O Joy! Felicitas!
Turn on the gas, and then – turn on the gas!
Let us go back to that benighted age
When *The Bohemian Girl* was all the rage.
When lawyers' lovely daughters took the air
In thy salubrious gardens, Mountjoy Square!
When Henrietta Street shone warm and bright
And carriages rolled castlewards at night.
When the tall fronts of North Great George's Street
Screened from the cold the sanctified elite.
When very few had ventured out as far
As pure Rathmines or, purer still, Rathgar.
Before my stage career had yet begun,
To cut it short – in 1871.
In 1871, this very night
The Dublin Gaiety first blazed with light.
Oh, let me try to reconstruct the scene –
Turn off the white light and turn on the green.
Ghosts! Silver ghosts of former players here
Around the auditorium appear.
There in the gallery I think I see
The sheeted wraith of Mr Beerbohm Tree.
Look! The dress circle! There the darkness tells
Of Henry Irving and the sound of Bells.
From yonder flat a breath as cold as clay
Blows Sarah Bernhardt here from yesterday.
In draughty passages behind the stage
Where gas jets flicker in a wiry cage,

Close by the dressing room 'mid greasepaint smells,
Lounge ghostly figures of Victorian swells.
They wait for Ellen Terry who will fling
A noble look and take the flowers they bring.
Ah, dear old Gaiety! How many a play
Like Martin Harvey's goes *The Only Way*.
Lost in the lumber of the past today
Old photographs can show, though faint and brown,
How Mrs Pat electrified the town
As Second Mrs Tanqueray. For me
Gone is the glory of what-used-to-be.
Only these floriated golden walls
Can recollect the hundred curtain calls
Of Hilda Moody's 'O Mimosa San'
In '97 when *The Geisha* ran,
And ask the branchy old electroliers
If Wilson Barnett moved the house to tears.
Ask the wide roof, did it the laughter hold
When, thirty years ago, the *Knights Were Bold*?
Did last war's audiences have enough
Of flighty plays – *A Little Bit of Fluff*?
And did old Dublin laugh to see such things
As *Lady Madcap, Bunty Pulls the Strings*?
Or did she like to keen a bit and grieve
With Walter Howard on his *Seven Days' Leave*?
Things pass so soon. I find I now forget
What were the song hits of *No, No, Nanette*.
No matter! Here since then I've been to see
An artist in a different line from me.
Ireland's great comic actor – James O'Dea.
And here's to Jimmy! Now's the time to say
The Gaiety is seventy today.

The grand old lady's living, kicking still,
Caesar and Cleopatra on her bill.
The great tradition she has known before
Goes on with Edwards and Mac Liammóir.

TO UFFINGTON RINGERS

Now it is Christmas, and that pollard stump
   Might be a willow over Rosy Brook;
   The blackened ivy has a Berkshire look;
Those moonlit beeches in a silver clump
Might shadow Weyland Smithy and the hump
   Of dear, familiar down, where once we took
   Schoolchildren picnics; until I forsook
Our parish for this other parish pump.

And here is Ireland, hemisphered in stars:
   High, lucky stars! you hang on Berkshire too,
     On brittle Christmas grass of Berkshire ground.
And fierce, above the moonlight, blazes Mars.
   Would, Berkshire ringers, I could wait with you
     To swing your starlit belfries into sound.

ROSEMARY HALL

Where the Massachusetts birches silver lean o'er Stanwick
    Road
    Stands the ancient Yandell homestead crammed with
        Sheraton and Spode;
Hope, the tomboy of the family, asked *Rosemarians* to tea
    (By permission of Miss Augur) every Sunday after
        three.

There it happened once in winter we were sitting idly by,
    Sallie Spahr (the Fire Lieutenant), Emmie, Fiskie,
        Muggs and I,
Talking over things Rosemarian when the Chaplain came
    to call,
    Just imagine! Father Terry waiting in the Yandell hall.
He was but the Reverend Terence Hanson de Montfort
    Gray,
    Yet my goodness! how he held our pure New England
        hearts in sway.
Pale, ascetic and consumptive, very, very, very high,
    We adored him, Sallie, Emmie, Fiskie, Muggs and
        Hope and I.

It was late in the semester, things were getting quite a bore,
    We were filled with false assurance, each a schoolgirl
        sophomore,
So we plotted to abduct him, make him marry then and
    there,
    Take his choice of us, the others would be bridesmaids
        to the pair.

Emmie had a lovely Packard, Fiskie had a dandy Dodge,
   Waiting, both, to take us schoolwards slow beside the
   Yandell lodge.

'Father Terry,' whispered Emmie, looking slant-eyed, fair
   and sweet,
   'We have got religion badly, and are off to a Retreat.
Miss Runty Rees says you can take us – travel in my
   Packard too –
   You're a cute Retreat conductor: will you chaperone us?
   Do.
There's a church in Berkshire County where the services
   are high;
   Come along at once with Sallie, Fiskie, Muggs and
   Hope and I.'

Father Terry looked embarrassed, Fiskie looked a bit
   annoyed,
   When he climbed in Emmie's Packard and her Dodge
   was not employed.
We had just got out of Greenwich when the Packard gave
   a jolt,
   Running over something furry which looked rather
   like a colt.
'Shall we stop?' said Muggs and Fiskie; 'Better not,' said
   Sallie Spahr;
   'It's a *horse*,' said Hope, 'oh heaven, what them bareback
   riders are!
Emmie's horse, Lieutenant!' so she braked, and Father
   Terry, he
   Blushed a lot when Fiskie, frightened, clambered up
   upon his knee.

Worst of horrors! we had stopped beside Rosemarian
    hockey grounds,
And the furry-coated figure was a woman, was Miss
    Lowndes.
We'd all of us forgotten, in the thrill of things, of course,
    That Miss Lowndes in her chinchilla looked extremely
    like a horse.

THE TAILWAGGERS' FRIEND

My four-footed friends, they bark all night:
Pungie, Nervy, Noisy and Bite.

At breakfast time like poisonous fungi
Passes the air from dear little Pungie.

A visitor comes and his ankle's tight
In the two-fanged teeth of dear old Bite.

When the telephone rings we're topsy-turvy:
Smash! yelp! clatter! goes great big Nervy.

When Master's away from his funny wee boysie,
High and prolonged moans shivering Noisy.

Oh, I'm the Tailwaggers' Friend, all right!
Pungie, Nervy, Noisy and Bite.

MARGATE, 1946

The terrace of houses that frames the Parade,
Though six years encrusted with stucco that's greyed,
Is courageously facing the salt-whetted wind
With the weather-scarred fishermen, rugged and kind.

The pier that stretched out with its finger of scorn
At an enemy coastline was damaged and torn,
But workmen are eager with present-day zest,
Disturbing the starlings from their strange jetty nest.

From Cecil Square, Hawley Street, Trinity Hill,
Ascending to see the church standing there still,
But closer inspection will nakedly tell
That Trinity Church is now only a shell.

Then, inviting to worship the folk far and near,
Come the bells of St John's, tintinnabuly clear,
And the gulls swooping in from the fishing-smack's prow
So greedily feather-fan round the spring plough.

With June will come visitors back to regain
Their health and vitality. Air like champagne
Will offer its sun-sparkling wealth to each one,
And the sands will re-echo to laughter and fun.

A MEMORY OF 1940

When father went out on his basic
   With Muriel, Shirley and me,
We drove up to somebody's mansion
   And asked them to give us some tea.

'Get out of that there, we're the workers.
   This mansion is ours, so to speak.
For Dad turns a handle at Sidcup
   At twenty-five guineas a week.

'I'm paid by the buffet at Didcot
   For insulting the passengers there.
The way they keep rattling the doorknob
   Disturbs me in doing my hair.

'And Shirley does crosswords at Dolcis
   (She's ever so clever at clues)
Plus twelve quid a week and her dinner
   For refusing the customers' shoes.

'And Muriel slaves at a laundry
   From ten-forty-five until four.
But the overtime rates were enormous,
   So she don't have to work any more.

'So get to hell out of that mansion,
   We workers have got all the tin,
And Dad has been promised a peerage
   When the Communist Party comes in.'

ABERDEEN

Farewell, Aberdeen, 'twixt the Donside and Deeside,
How oft have I strayed through the long summer day.
On the fringe of the links o'er the wide-spreading seaside
To see the pink pebbles caressed by the spray.

How gay as a student by King's rugged steeple
I loitered in archways and meadow paths green.
To my Jacobite sympathies kind were the people
Though deep in Balmoral dwelt Hanover's Queen.

From windows of dreamland I see the grey granite,
All sparkling with diamonds after the rain,
The Dee and the arch and suspensions that span it
And fir-covered forests that rise from the plain.

Down Union Street with majestical motion
Electrical tramcars go painted in green.
The ships to thy quaysides come in from the ocean,
But I leave forever my loved Aberdeen.

IN OVERCLIFFE

In Overcliffe, it was in Overcliffe
    That Peter shyly showed me first his trains,
Perched on that turf and thymy clover cliff
    While down below the seaweed stank like drains.
A warm and blustering sou'wester shook
The bellows hanging in the inglenook.

Red velveteen I wore, red velveteen,
    Mummy's magenta lipstick on my lips.
My hair was all fluffed out, fluffed out with Drene.
    I smiled a little, and I swung my hips,
But he said nothing as he held the door
Except 'The rest are out till half-past four.'

OCTOBER BELLS

On this wide October morning when the air is full of
      church bells,
    Four from Hitcham, six from Burnham, and from
      Slough and Taplow eight,
When the ground is red with dying of the gentle leaves of
      chestnuts,
    Why is Mother smoking Players, why does Father get
      up late?
    Why the milk unclaimed on doorsteps all along the
      new estate?

Dark below the orange beeches glow the box trees and
      the holly,
    And how gold the silent oaktops clustered in the steel
      blue air,
And the woodlands pop and crackle shedding husks and
      nuts and acorns,
    Squashed on tarmac, drowned in puddles, lost in leaf
      mould anywhere.
    What a loving waste of fruitage, not that Mum and
      Daddy care.

Bermondsey gas was bright in a very Low Church in
    Nunhead
(The which, despite its names, is a Protestant part of
    London).
Forward I bent in my pew, shading my eyes and waiting
For the minister (*not* a priest who sacrifices at altars)
To give the blessing, when oh! such a pyrotechnic explosion:
Saxons and mines and serpents, and Roman (shame of
    them!) candles,
Catherine wheels and rockets and that illegal mixture
Made of potassium chlorate and sulphide of arsenic,
    bursting
Like benefit night at the Palace when seen from Penge or
    Anerley,
Quite overwhelmed my sense. I clung to the gas jet standard
Ordered by Mr Vulliamy – I'm an architect by profession –
From Skidmore & Son of Coventry, ecclesiastical ironwork.
I clung to the standard believing that stained-glass
    windows by Hardman
Had let themselves out of their lights and were whirling
    about before me.
My fellow church warden started. I took one look at a
    capital,
Dear old Middle-Pointed (I've done much better you'll
    notice,
Although in a later style in my work for the Corporation),
I took one look at the cap and one at my fellow church
    warden.

So this was the world! Goodbye! I glanced at the Holy
    Table,
Thankful even in death to see no Eastward position,
And then I was where I am, communicating to you, sir,
Through the medium of Mr Betjeman, poetaster and
    poet,
Who possibly understands the loss of the world I lived in,
Here by my windy graveside. I am buried in Norwood
    cemetery.

THE WEARY JOURNALIST

Here on this far North London height
I sit and write and write and write;
I pull the nothings from my head
And weight them round with lumps of lead
Then plonk them down upon the page
In finely simulated rage.
Whither Democracy? I ask,
And What the Nature of her Task?
Whither Bulgaria and Peru?
What Crisis are they passing through?
Before my readers can reply
Essential Factors flutter by;
Parlous, indeed, is their condition
Until they find a Key Position.
To keep their Tendencies in Check
I push them through a Bottleneck
From which they Challenge me and frown
And Fling their Tattered Gauntlets down,
And Vital Problems sit and trill
Outside upon my window sill,
And Lies are wrapped around in Tissues
And oh! the crowds of Vital Issues.
I ache in all my mental joints
Nigh stabbed to death by Focal Points.
But all the time I know, I know
That every twinkling light below
Shines on a Worker in his Vest
(True symbol of the Great Oppressed)
And he, like all unheeding fools,
Is filling in his football pools.

THE DEATH OF THE UNIVERSITY READER OF SPANISH

The Colonel lies upon his bed
And rests his dear old cube-shaped head.
Above him, hanging in the frieze,
Is carved the crest of the MAGEES,
While underneath him there is not
The vestige of a Chamber-pot,
Because *the Colonel*, you must know,
Is subject to no overflow.
The food he eats is desiccated
And subsequently sublimated,
And so is he, and that is how
He comes to be where he is now.

SODA is lying on the 'couch'
And so is FRED and so is SOUCH.
There is an air in every room
At least of Thought, if not of Gloom.
The Carpets shiver to themselves,
The Plates are silent on the shelves
(And some of them are very old
And some of them are not, I'm told).
The toothbrushes in order ranged
And all remarkably unchanged
(And these are older far in date
Than any rug or any plate).
The bits of sponge of various shades,
The fifty years of razor blades,
And these no evidence betray
That 'tis *the Colonel*'s dying day.

She only mourns, the Dame TRALEES,
Beside the bed of the MAGEES.

What glimpse of the Eternal flashes
Across those long mascara-ed lashes?
What meetings with the blessed dead
Await that dear old cube-shaped head?
See like a spark from ETNA's crater
The everlasting soul of PATER.
It flits about the room and rests
Beside *the Colonel*'s woollen vests.
And what is that thing over there
With neither face nor form nor hair,
Just disembodied Intellect?
It's dear old PLATO, I expect.
It has departed by itself
To browse about the Youth Club shelf,
Till hark! a roll of Heavenly Drums,
The King of all, MAX PLOWMAN comes.
'Welcome, old friend,' MAX PLOWMAN cries,
And with a smile, *the Colonel* dies.

'And now that you have got your wings,
Let's test the Actualness of things.
Here, PLATO, what say you to this? –
Does that "Become" which yet not "Is"?
Can the intrinsic "Is"-potential
Invalidate the non-Essential?
Sed hoc, quod miles, Alma mater,
Elaborate the thesis, PATER.
Come, KOLKHORST, help untie the Tangle!
WE'VE ALL ETERNITY TO WRANGLE.'

Oh what a joy, *the Colonel* finds,
It is to be with First Class minds.
Instead of silly sexy patter
He joins in things that Really Matter.
As PATER, PLATO, PLOWMAN talk
He goes on Endless Country Walk
Along the bare *Elysian Fields*
Where not a Dog its Nuisance yields.

But she, poor luckless Mortal here,
The DAME TRELEASE lets fall a tear.
She gazes on the Corpse and sighs
And puts some pennies on its eyes,
And then tiptoe-ing down the stairs
Sees Honest TOBY at his prayers
And FATHER HUGH beside him kneeling,
Both overcome by decent feeling.

Before them lying white and still,
Behold *the Newly-Opened Will*.

1.

See here the north of England shown
Before the factory towns had grown,
A rugged land and little known:
Stone cottages and dales and hills,
Brown streams and clacking water-mills,
And gradually into it
The railways brought their soot and grit.

2.

Until today this land you see
Transformed by heavy industry.
There's country still – but in-between
The close-packed towns of the machine.
Coal mines and chimneys, tips and dumps,
A worrying land of booms and slumps,
And all the time the houses spread
In endless lines of brick-built red.
They house hard-working people who
Are better perhaps than me and you.

3.

[*The filmstrip shows the General Secretary of the Additional Curates Society at his writing desk, looking worried because of the mounting appeals from vicars for grants to pay for curates.*]
And who's that person sitting there,
His ageing features lined with care?
It is not very hard to guess –
The Secretary of the A.C.S.

His letters, thirty a day at least,
All ask for stipends for a priest
To come and lend a helping hand
In our too overcrowded land.

4.
Just read the lines he's holding here,
And then the problem will appear.
Great Kirkby's an industrial place
And growing at a frightening pace.
Well, I'll stop talking while you read
About its Vicar's urgent need.
[*The filmstrip shows a letter from a vicar that reads 'I have
a town parish of 25,000 people, and there is also the Great
Kirkby building estate going up. It has 10,000 people at pres-
ent, 600 are coming in each week, and there is no church on
the estate. These people have never had a chance; they only
live for the pools, the pub, the dogs, and the cinema. Single-
handedly I cannot hope to convert my people. I have two
curates who can come to me in three months' time, but with-
out the help of the A.C.S. I cannot definitely appoint them.'*]

5.
And there's great Kirkby: you can see
The old church – 1843
I think's the year when it was built.
But now the town has 'overspilt'
(To use a smart town-planning phrase)
Since Queen Victoria's early days,
And factories, with their smoke and roar,
Rise where were pleasant fields before.
Great Kirkby has to emigrate . . .

6.

. . . To live upon this new estate.
Oh yes, it's up to date, all right.
The cinema's a lovely sight;
The fine slap-up department store
Thrills Mrs Ackroyd to the core.
There are petrol pumps and private cars
And sumptuous mock-Tudor bars.
In the new streets you'll also see
That everybody's got TV.

7.

Physical wants are well supplied,
But not the soul deep down inside.
The church is out of date, they say,
And anyhow it's miles away.
And so Great Kirkby's young folk are
Married before a Registrar.
The vicar's way back in the town,
Too far to take the babies down
To be baptised, and really all
We want him for's a funeral.
Our children now are truly free
From any Christianity,
And if they go to Borstal – well,
There isn't God, or Heaven or Hell.
Religion's only for the rich . . .

8.

. . . But things have got to such a pitch
Within the Ackroyd family,
That this nice breakfast scene you see:

A hangover hangs over Dad,
He says the sausages are bad.
Wilf's late for work, can't stop to eat,
He's making off into the street
In fearful dudgeon, and oh my,
Just see the pattern on his tie.
I wish his face was half as bright –
And as for Mum, the tea's not right,
And nothing's right, oh poor old Mum,
No wonder she is looking glum.

9.
Wilf sees no harm, as some folk do,
In 'knocking off' a thing or two.
Here are some wood and tools he's taking
For a bike shed that he's making.

10.
Hurrah! The foreman's going out.
There's nobody in charge about,
So Wilf decides to join his mate
At housey-housey while they wait.
Perhaps the luck will come his way
And right his loss of yesterday.

11.
And now the welcome evening's come,
A time of rest, but not for Mum;
For Dad is going to the pub,
And Wilf is going to the club,
And neither of them ever wishes
To help old mother with the dishes.

12.

And this is just as we have found her,
With all the dirty crockery round her,
Resolving to go round and see
Old Auntie Green and drink some tea;
For Auntie's got an occult way
Of telling what the tea-leaves say.

13.

And here she is with Auntie Green,
Oh! what an edifying scene.
'I see a stranger dressed in black.
Be warned by me, he's on your track.'
And Mum is answering, 'Get away,
Whatever will my hubby say?'

14.

Now from this old church in the town
The Sunday bell is ringing down:
'Parish Communion half-past-nine',
And some folk go there wet or fine.

15.

But not so Wilf, he settles deep
Into his Sunday morning sleep,
And that alarm clock on the shelf
Is only ringing to itself.

16.

At twelve he mounts his motorbike
And takes a girl he seems to like;
And with a roaring detonation,
He shocks the Matins congregation.

17.

And now because the A.C.S.
Has helped the Vicar in distress
And sent a curate to him, we
Can watch their plan of action. 'See,'
The Vicar says, 'You run the show
Here in the *old* church; I must go
And reach, if it is not too late,
The people on the new estate!'

18.

Four months go by, and then one day,
As Dad and Wilf are on their way
From work, they see to their surprise
Their Vicar playing at mud-pies,
They think – until they realise
That he is really trying to build
A church up here. To say they're thrilled
Would not be true, but all the same
They stop and watch his little game.
The vicar is a cunning man;
To catch the Ackroyds is his plan.
He knows their names, he knows their trade,
He loves his people, and he's prayed
For all of them and got to know
About their lives. He says, 'Hullo.
Well, Mr Ackroyd, how d'you do?
I'm wanting some advice from you;
As you're a joiner, come and see
This timber. And if you agree
That it is good, I'd like to use
It for the panelling and pews.'

19.
Well, Dad's delighted to advise.
He talks at length and argufies
On mitres, mortices and joints,
And various other knotty points,
And even Wilf is pleased to hear . . .

20.
. . . They all go in the pub for beer.
The vicar says, 'Next Sunday I
A new experiment will try.
At nine o'clock then there will be
Communion in a house, and we
Can meet at Mrs Jenkins's.
The only thing that's missing is
Accompaniment for when we sing.'
And someone pipes up, 'Dad can bring
His squeeze-box.' Mr Ackroyd flushes,
And in his pint-pot hides his blushes.

21.
On Sunday morning, see them then
Gathered around, just nine or ten.
And Mr Ackroyd's present too,
Playing his squeeze-box good and true.

22.
The hymn tunes all his memory fire
Of days when he was in the choir,
A little boy. And even on Monday
He thinks he'll come along next Sunday.

23.

*[The filmstrip shows the vicar visiting Mrs Ackroyd and
asking if she has a Bible for that evening's home meeting.
She sheepishly removes a potted plant from the family Bible,
which is being used as a plant stand.]*
Now why had Mum that sheepish look
As this nice ornament she took? –
Just read the name upon the book.

24.

I think that one good reason why
About religion we are shy
Is not so much because we doubt it
But that we don't know much about it.
The vicar is a friendly man,
He talks to Mum as few folks can,
And shows her what he's preaching on
Out of the Gospel of St John.

25.

The Vicar now extends his teaching
By taking up street-corner preaching.
Some people say he is a fool;
Some say he thinks it's Sunday School.
But others like the Ackroyds stay
And learn about the Christian way.
Neighbours come in from far and near
The parson's discourses to hear
On how we ought to live and why
Our Lord came down on earth to die
And rose again and conquered Death.
He talks to them about the Faith,

He talks about the Sacraments.
They seem to think he's talking sense.
You'll see that Wilf is in the throng,
And he has brought his girl along.

CLAY AND SPIRIT

Yellow November flowering ivy,
    Penned-up sheep and the stacked-up hay,
Crested gold over purple scrubland
    Elm trees rot in a still decay.

Water rushes through limestone arches,
    Whirls the leaves a parish away,
'One, two, three,' in a fungus odour,
    The bellcote summons for All Saints' Day.

'One, two, three,' to a cold stone chancel,
    Two small lights and a priest to pray;
Humming machines on a misty landscape
    Drown the sound of the soaking clay.

Out of the clay the saints were moulded,
    Out of the clay the Wine and Bread,
But out of the soul the heart that withers,
    As brains increase in the big white head.

I wish you could meet our delightful archdeacon,
There is not a thing he's unable to speak on.
And if what he says does not seem to you clear,
You will have to admit he's extremely sincere.

Yes, he is a man with his feet on the ground;
His financial arrangements are clever and sound.
I find as his bishop I'm daily delighted
To think of the livings his skill has united.

Let me take for example St Peter the Least
Which was staffed by a most irresponsible priest.
There are fewer less prejudiced persons than I,
But the services there were impossibly High.

Its strange congregation was culled from afar,
And you know how eclectic such worshippers are.
The stipend was small but the site was worth more
Than any old church I have sold here before.

I'm afraid its supporters were apt to forget
The crippling extent of diocesan debt,
Though our able archdeacon explained to them all
Of his reasons for selling their church and their hall.

I'm a moderate man and averse to extremes,
So St George's was hardly the church of my dreams.
It was Classic in style and most needlessly Low,
And we felt that, in fairness, it too ought to go.

With the sum the archdeacon obtained for the site
And its very rich living, we now can unite
St George and St Peter and see them again
In a moderate church I've allowed to remain –

A worshipful place which I greatly admire
For the length of its chancel and tone of its choir,
And I've promised to preach them a course during Lent
On How the Diocesan Quota is Spent.

THE ST PAUL'S APPEAL

I've turned from Queen Victoria Street
    Down gas-lit lanes on windy nights
To where the wharves and water meet
    And seen the sliding river lights,
And looked through Georgian window panes
    At plasterwork in City halls,
While dominant and distant reigns,
    Queen of the sky, the dome of Paul's.

Young clerks with cheeks of boyish rose
    In bars and cafés underground,
Old clerks who play at dominoes
    Where cigarette smoke hangs around,
Girl secretaries eating beans
    In restaurants with white-tiled walls –
They all know what the City means,
    They all are children of St Paul's.

Directors who with eyes shut fast
    Are driven Esher-wards at three,
And those who leave the City last,
    Gay members of some livery
Looking in vain for cab or bus
    Down cobbled lanes where moonlight falls –
The first and last to leave of us
    Are brooded over by St Paul's.

If in some City church we've knelt,
    Shut off from traffic noise and news,

And all the past about us felt
   Among the cedar-scented pews,
Or if we think the past is rot,
   Or if our purse has other calls,
Whether we go to church or not,
   Which of us will not help St Paul's?

THE DIVINE SOCIETY

Oh, many a parson I have known
And one perhaps is like your own,
So listen carefully while I
Run through a few from Low to High,
From Fathers cared for by their sisters
To heavily moustachioed misters,
And leaveners of the mighty lump,
The moderates of the middle stump.
  The Reverend Father Cyprian Spike
Is just the sort of man I like.
He's fond of claret and a joke,
His church is blue with incense smoke,
His daily celebrations said
In vestments green, black, gold or red;
On Sundays they're superbly sung
(And some say in the Latin tongue).
Though critics think his ways are odd
Still underneath's a man of God
Who prays for, meets and loves his flock,
Whose Faith is stalwart as a rock.
Large-hearted, if a bit dogmatic,
He's brave and gentle, yet emphatic.
  His curate is, to say the least,
Rather too markedly the priest,
Ascetic, cold, austere and shy,
He will grow mellower by and by
But never, surely, quite so mellow
As that extremely jovial fellow.
  Too breezy, back-slapping and hearty
To be connected with a party –

The old sky pilot, sporty Chubb,
Who's frightfully good in church and pub.
'The Lord be with you', 'All the best',
Are uttered with an equal zest.
He likes his pipe, he's good with men
Who meet for chinwags in his den.
He runs a flourishing men's society
Which has a genuine kind of piety.
The faith of many a rugger tough
Is proof that Sporty knows his stuff,
For through the pipe smoke and the show,
A love of souls burns bright below.
    Archdeacon Diocese is one
Whose life to me seems much less fun,
Though he undoubtedly enjoys
His multifarious employs,
Devising schemes from deep researches
For making cash by selling churches,
Re-organising that and this.
'Without Archdeacon Diocese,'
Our bishop says, 'I would be lost.'
The parish knows this to its cost.
The Archdeacon's parish rarely sees him
Since conferences always please him.
He's always off to distant cities
To sit on grandly named committees.
His wife declares he gets all trembly
The week before the Church Assembly.
This is a nice thing to recall,
It shows he's human after all.
    How different he from Squarson Tomb,
Rector and Squire of Tiddlecombe.

He never leaves his parish bounds
Except when hunting with the hounds.
His services are just the same
As fifty years back when he came.
How different, too, is Mr Chores,
All Ritualism he abhors,
All ritual, at any rate,
Except the raising of the plate
At Morning Prayer, and he would rather
Be called by any name but 'Father'.
His wife and family think the same,
And 'Daddy' is his household name.
But he is earnest, good and kind,
You'd have to go for miles to find
A man who'd take such pains to win
Your soul from misery and sin.
And though he does not hear Confessions,
He'll talk you out of your transgressions.
Yes, Mr Chores's a man I like,
And friendly too with Father Spike.
    But what's so wonderful to me
Is all these men are C of E.
And when I hear how people blame
The Church for not being all the same,
I tell them just to keep in mind
How God created human kind.
He didn't have a single mould,
But what he did was really bold:
He planned to have a rich variety
Within his one Divine Society,
And that Society for me
Is the warm and friendly C of E.

VILLAGE WEDDING

In summer wind the elm leaves sing,
    And sharp's the shade they're shedding,
And loud and soft the church bells ring
    For Sally Weaver's wedding.

With chasing light the meadows fill,
    The greenness growing greener,
As racing over White Horse Hill
    Come bluer skies and cleaner.

The chalk-white walls, the steaming thatch
    In rain-washed air are clearing,
And waves of sunshine run to catch
    The bride for her appearing.

Inside the church in every pew
    Sit old friends, older grown now;
Their children whom our children knew
    Have children of their own now.

The babies wail, the organ plays,
    Now thunderous, now lighter;
The brightest day of Sally's days
    Grows every moment brighter.

And all the souls of Uffington,
    The dead among the living,
Seem witnessing the rite begun
    Of taking and of giving.

The flying clouds! the flying years!
  The church of centuries seven!
How new its weathered stone appears
  When vows are made in Heaven!

Up! leap up! then *down*, and into the alder'd surface
Where ferrying water boatmen skim on the calm cathe-
    dral,
And billows of elm and cloud go rippling over the mill
    pond.
Up! leap! then *down* from the warm blue summer of
    Wiltshire.
God, what limbs I had! What a glorious athlete's figure!
I struck out strong for the bank where my father, the
    miller, in gaiters
Looked across August fields for ducks coming into the
    barley.
He was the spirit of England, and I was the heir to his
    fortune –
The rumbling stones and the leat and the antiquated
    machinery,
The new Rolls Royce in the yard, and here was my dainty
    mother
Holding a towel to dry my wonderful athlete's body.
I was perfect in all respects except for my wretched
    eyesight.

The county looked down on the close, the close looked
    down on the city.
I felt it even then, the essential slight to my mother.
She was ground in the social cogs before I realised father
Was little more than a brute with his uncontrollable
    temper,

His farming cronies, his snooker, and regrettable
  Wiltshire accent.
No wonder we weren't invited to tea in the canons'
  houses,
Though, goodness knows, my mother was just as much of
  a lady
As any clergyman's wife with hardly a penny to bless her
And gawky sons at a day school or Monkton Combe or
  Lancing,
While I was going to Marlborough and richer than them
  and better,
If it weren't for my wretched eyesight and vulgar brute of
  a father.

Why do I look like a sheep? I have brains, ability, morals.
I swim for my house. I tolerate those above and below
  me.
I can read, without being shocked, the novels of Aldous
  Huxley
And Inge's *Outspoken Essays*. I specialise in history.
The man who teaches us art (though he hasn't my mental
  equipment)
Praises the way in my paintings I catch the spirit of
  Wiltshire.
It's a pity the school is run by a junta of philistine masters
Attracted, it seems, by toughs who can play for their side
  in a house match
While I with exceptional gifts should really be senior
  prefect,
If it weren't for my brute of a father, my looks, and my
  wretched eyesight.

Time brought a splendid revenge: I confounded them all
    with my brilliance
When after a visit to Oxford and gruelling history viva
I won the Brackenbury scholarship, best of its year, into
    Balliol.
Such was my power of phrase and masterly grasp of the
    subject –
'Russia herself flung down to Poland the tattered gauntlet
While Metternich's tottering power left Austria Europe's
    lackey.'
I went to the town to send a telegram off to my mother.
Then what had Marlborough left to offer a Balliol
    scholar?
Masters and boys alike were essentially second-raters
Holding me down like my father, my looks and my
    wretched eyesight.

I suppose that on glancing back I can say that my terms at
    Oxford
In those early halcyon days were indescribably foolish.
I, with my first-class brains and respectable Wiltshire
    background,
Consorted with those below me in every respect but
    income.
Benjamin Rudolph Bonas, the son of a diamond broker,
Gave me the best champagne, for which I still have a
    liking,
Oysters and caviar. Yes, he was my evil genius.
So, in a lesser sense, were those I pursued for their bodies
(Very few first-rate bodies have first-rate brains inside
    them).
Their lithe provocative limbs so hindered my concentration

123

I left with a double third for which I must blame Ben
    Bonas,
My unfortunate taste for the fleshpots, my father, my
    looks, and my eyesight.

There flows in my blood a sense of the world's continuing
    history
Running like grassy tracks on the downs of my native
    Wiltshire.
Out of the Stone to the Bronze Age and on to the Celts
    and Romans,
And so to the fertile Saxons with their Witenagemots and
    Hundreds,
Through Norman and Mediæval to the sturdy
    Elizabethans.
I can trace my ancestry back from Gervase Bowle of
    Devizes,
Whose arms, a spear impaling a *poisson d'or* pursuivant,
Are in my mother's sitting room now. This was better
    than Bonas
And very much better than Betjeman, whose quite
    untraceable forbears
Were probably peddling hashish in the marts of Asia
    Minor
When buccaneering Bowle received the rent of his
    manor.
A shrewd old Wiltshireman he, who cast his lot with the
    Roundheads.
Well, it's all tremendous fun if it weren't for the probings
    of pedants
Who think that their firsts and seconds are grounds for
    doubting my findings.

The state I was left in now was absurd, unfair and ridiculous.
My first-class brains lay fallow for want of a decent position
Editing *Time & Tide* or an academic appointment.
And father's behaviour to mother was inexcusably brutal.
So I felt I must get her away from his uncontrollable rages.
His business itself was failing through his usual incompetent bungling.
He refused me a decent allowance, and what he paid out to my mother
Was hardly enough for us both, so I had to augment our small income
And succeeded, by pulling strings, in obtaining a post as a master
In a fairly successful school where I wasted my time in teaching
Which should have been spent in research as a history fellow of Balliol.
The boys were attractive enough, but my colleagues of course were impossible.

The public-school teaching profession is wretchedly paid to begin with,
The only position worth having being that at the top – a headmaster.
And one way of muscling in on this tiresome headmaster-ship racket
Which I contemplated myself was the taking of Anglican orders.
Though this might mean passing exams, one could square them all right with one's conscience,

A few stock questions and answers, and very firm affirm-
   ations.
It ought to be easy enough. Another way up was to marry
The daughter of someone with power in the world of
   scholastic appointments.
She needn't be much to look at, but I had to think about
   mother,
Who had given up all to be with me; and a further snag
   to my marriage
Would be if I were asked to fulfil the physical part of the
   bargain.
I was really meant for a don and the talk and the port at
   high table.

1962

I ate the wilting chicory leaf
    In the dining car's Festival grey,
And I thought of Lord Bridges and Civil Servants
    And how they had come to stay.

The expense accounts dinner beyond me
    (On the rates of Stockton-on-Tees)
Had claret and hock. Oh, they're in for a shock
    If they want to be C.B.E.'s.

For mine is a lemon barley
    And I'm already a knight.
Festina lente since nineteen-twenty,
    It doesn't pay to be tight.

PROLOGUE SPOKEN BY PEGGY ASHCROFT AT
THE OPENING OF THE PEGGY ASHCROFT
THEATRE, CROYDON, 5 NOVEMBER 1962

Fellow citizens of Croydon, I am proud tonight to stand
In this new and splendid theatre, something to replace
    The Grand
(Family Circle two-and-sixpence, 'Croydon
    double-one-one-two',
And the Hippodrome – remember? – variety and light
    revue).

Standing here I still recall the Corporation Tramway ride
Out of Norbury to Purley, by the willowy Wandle side.
Madame Felton (late of Bond Street) gave our mothers
    Marcel waves,
The Café Royal provided banquets, Mr J B Shakespeare –
    graves.

Little did I as a schoolgirl, all those many years ago,
As I wandered where the Wandle does municipally flow,
Think there'd ever be a theatre which would take its
    name from me,
As I watched the Whitgift boys, walking home to prep
    and tea.

In those many years our theatres suffered loss and stress
    and strain.
Down they tumbled in their hundreds! Were they to be
    built again?

Steaming Odeons, scented Plazas, plushy Ritzes filled the
  void,
And the millions took to watching life in terms of celluloid.

Croydon steals a march on London, Croydon pioneers
  indeed:
Three halls – for music, painting, drama – answer an
  eternal need.
Theatre is a form of giving. Croydon, I give thanks to
  thee
For having named this noble theatre, after proud, unworthy
  me.

A GOOD INVESTMENT

The castor oil plant was the wife's idea.
Yes, that's her portrait that Bassano took,
Those are the kids there in the leather frame –
Do take it down and have a closer look.
Never mind that calendar, I've plenty more.
Though Jennifer has got a look of me,
The boy takes rather after his mamma.
He's down for Winchester. Some hopes, say I:
We're not a family much endowed with brains.
I'm not complaining, though, things might be worse.
Prestige block rents weren't what we could afford
In those pre-war days in St Mary Axe,
But, man, it's paid – not just for the address,
But merging with the Peter Woffin Group,
Then taking in Prefabroplasticoid.
With one well-oiled administrator
Doing the work of three in half the time,
It cut our overheads by eighty-five per cent
Even in the first year when we settled in.
You can't afford to wait, you can't stand still;
It's either chuck your hand in or expand.
Now let me get you something. Miss Trefane,
The key of the hospitality cabinet, please –
In Major Plumpton's room, I saw it last.

ST MARY'S CHAPEL OF EASE

Believe me, IDOLATRY ne'er shall invade
That splendid parabola's sanctified shade,
Which shall rise in its silence forbidding and dark
As it did o'er the childhood of Austin O'Clarke.
For now that the POPE is becoming I.C.
With vernacular masses and Wilson to tea,
The Ecumenist leap is so light o'er the wall
That the Black Church's pinnacles never need fall.
The stone shall proclaim in the loudest of hymns,
'McQUAID is at last in communion with SIMMS.'

THE FINEST WORK IN ENGLAND: I. K. BRUNEL

From Normandy in France my father came,
My father Marc Brunel, to make his name
Here by the Thames's wide slow-flowing shore,
To build a tunnel never known before.
At Wapping deep the entrance shafts he sank
From which to burrow to the Surrey bank,
A brick-lined passageway defying mud,
Thames quicksand, gravel, sewage, ooze and flood.
Defying flood? My father Marc Brunel
And I his son who helped him couldn't tell
What was to happen next. When tides were high
Our tunnel flooded. But we pumped it dry
And then we gave, from fears of flood released,
London's – the world's – first underwater feast.
Short was our triumph. In the water came,
Wrecking the tunnel and my father's name.
I, Isambard, his son henceforth must stand
Alone to conquer rivers, oceans, land.

I went to Bristol for a breath of air
After that foul Thames water. Gazing there
Across the Avon gorge I saw a span
Of height and depth as yet uncrossed by man.
Contemptible seemed bridge designs to me
By older men – for I was twenty-three.
Their schemes to cross the forge looked out of place,
Lacking imagination, force and grace.
I made my own in the Egyptian style,
A memory at Clifton of the Nile.

Needless to say with my design I won.
Bristol, all hail! With you my fame begun.

Those dreamy docks, that lambent waterside,
St Mary Redcliffe sleeping in the tide.
Bristol was losing in the race for trade
To giant strides that Liverpool had made.
Her surest route to London – waterway:
The locks through Bath alone took half a day,
Slowly through meadows, slow up Wiltshire downs,
By sleeping fields and sleepier country towns –
The Kennet and Avon for its day was fine,
But not so sure and fast a link as mine.
I would join Bristol by an iron road.
In new Egyptian style my arches strode.
The Wharncliffe viaduct across the Brent
Westward from London on its journey went.
A hundred years of merchandise and men
Have crossed my flat-arched viaduct since then.
Ours was a seven-foot gauge – our track was wide.
Long, straight and smooth it crossed the countryside,
Wider and faster than a coach or cart –
Triumph of engineering and of art.
Through marshy Middlesex and on to Bucks –
London to Bristol linked by lines of trucks.
People opposed us – landlords, mayors, MPs,
They called the railway mania a disease.
And so my fine Great Western came to rest
At Taplow first and waited to go west.
Eton's headmaster thought my railway's noise
Would lure to London all his bashful boys,
So he objected – as you might suppose.

At Maidenhead still more contention rose.
The turnpike people, loss of tolls their dread,
Objected to my railway bridge. They said
The flat brick arches wouldn't stand the strain
Of cart or carriage, let alone a train.
How wrong they were. How loyal were my men.
The great Great Western service founded then
Has kept alive since 1839
The living reputation of the line.
A railway service like a ship at sea
Depends upon its crew. These men to me
Were life and blood, were maintenance and crew.
They built the line and from them my strength I drew.
That Sonning cutting was an awkward bit.
One bank kept sliding down – we planted it
At Reading where canal and river meet.
I crossed my rival and my bridge was neat.

And now the plain of Berkshire open lies,
Arable acres under flying skies.
Each mile was turbulent of my survey.
Landlords and farmers argued rights of way
Till, arguing done, I laid my iron trail
Down through the middle of the White Horse Vale.
I sketched, I surveyed, kept the rustics calm,
Telling them railways brought them wealth, not harm.
In many a wretched inn I stayed the night,
In many a country church I took delight,
And built our houses at the halfway mile
At Steventon in local Tudor style.
How many a journey on my mare I made
Before that broad-gauge track was truly laid.

And so the line to Bristol nearer drew,
And over half my mighty task was through.
Stations I built to suit the countryside
Of local stone, foursquare, verandahed wide,
And this is how they looked when in their pride.

The Company's offices in Tudor style
I built at Bristol's Temple Meads meanwhile.
Bristol, which gave my great Great Western birth,
Should have the finest wooden roof on earth.
Over its terminus and still today
That same roof shelters a neglected bay
In the same spot. We will draw out, my friend,
And watch the progress from the Bristol end.

We cut through cliffs. My tunnel mouths I formed
Like Norman castles waiting to be stormed.
Bridges were outer walls across my path,
And so I pierced the hills to Roman Bath.

Bath station front recalled a Tudor past:
'Twas once like Bristol, wooden roofed and vast,
But when I came to lay the track outside
I thought of Bath in all her Georgian pride,
And Roman-looking was my cutting deep
Leading from Wiltshire – churches, elms and sheep.
A railway should be simple, I maintain,
And unobtrusive as a country lane
Or monumental. Thus at Chippenham I
Raised it on arches, Roman plain and high,
Since much defaced. But now I well recall
We reached the greatest obstacle of all –
That hill at Box. I saw its limestone slope

And knew a tunnel was my only hope.
A two-mile tunnel – how could it be done?
I saw those gravestones in the Wiltshire sun:
Here in Box village men had worked in stone
For generations. I must raise my own
Strong band of quarrymen. One hundred died
Carving this cavern from the hill's inside
Where rocks came tumbling down to crush and kill
And water poured the quarryings to fill.
We finished it in 1841,
And thus was ended what we had begun,
And the completion of my grand design
I celebrated with an entrance fine –
London to Bristol linked by railway line.

My broad-gauge trains! Design, upkeep, repair
I soon assigned to Daniel Gooch's care,
A dour North countryman, my quiet friend
Who worked beside me loyal to the end.
Near Swindon Gooch laid out to my design
Works one side, houses t'other side the line
With gardens round them, drying grounds and parks,
And their own church by Gilbert Scott, St Mark's.
Workers in foundry, yard, repairing shed,
From these trim cottages their race was bred.
They brought the words 'Great Western' into fame,
Adding new lustre to old Swindon's name.
A friendly family grown large since then,
Proud to be thought of as Great Western men,
And in the works – they called the works 'inside' –
Turning out splendid engines was their pride.
Their work demanded long-experienced skill.

Let cold administration have its will,
They were 'Great Western' and they are so still.
Father to son, their skill was handed down.
Swindon remains at heart a railway town.

Swindon with Gooch! I realised my dream.
We conquered England by the power of steam,
And by the sad canal's defeated side
I looked with pity upon fallen pride.
Lost hopes upon the water! There remained
The final triumph that my father gained.
Insolvency, contempt and danger past,
His great Thames tunnel was complete at last.
Mighty rejoicings! souvenirs and bells!
Hailed for his genius! visited by swells!
And finally created bachelor knight
To soothe his failing frame. I was all right,
Never felt better. From my drawing board
A constant stream of inspiration poured –
A huge conservatory, cast iron and glass,
Over a cutting, thus there came to pass,
By little sketches, each improved upon,
My London Terminus at Paddington.
Scene of arrivals and farewells and tears,
How elegantly still it wears its years.
But what's a train for Bristol only bound?
With steam and iron I'll gird the world around.

Start slow at first. By Temple Meads you see
My handsome office for the B & E
(Bristol & Exeter). I built their track,
Broad-gauge of course, and flung across its back

This handsome bridge near Weston-super-Mare.
And Exeter – I had a failure there.
From here, my Exeter St Thomas station:
The line, I fear, went into liquidation.
No finer stretch of railway can be seen
Than this between the rivers Exe and Teign.
The broadening Exe, the mild South Devon air,
The smell of salt and seaweed everywhere.
That atmospheric railway scheme of mine
As a conception was extremely fine,
And had it worked the force of vacuum power
Would have drawn trains at eighty miles an hour
Without a sound along this Devon shore,
A rate of motion unattained before.
Its pumping stations I designed to be
Italian palaces beside the sea.
When I have had an extra glass of wine
I mourn the Devon atmospheric line.
But for what purposes is money lent
Except to make a bold experiment?
When I abandoned hope the tensions eased,
So I went back to steam and Gooch was pleased.

Through the red sandstone cliffs my track was good,
Subject of course to heavy seas and flood.
But oh, *mon dieu!* with Newton Abbot passed
I thought I'd met my Waterloo at last.
Those southwest Devon hills – beyond the river
Impossible valleys: nothing level ever.
I smoked cigars. They kept away the midges
As in despair I stood on ancient bridges
And thought of floods from Dartmoor rushing down,

Miles from a village, let alone a town.
Nature all around me: Plymouth unattained,
And universal torrents when it rained.
And this was how I spanned each deep ravine,
This was my contribution to the scene –
Stone piers supporting viaducts of wood,
And while they lasted they were strong and good.

At length I saw the Tamar broader far
Than Somerset or Devon rivers are.
Already I had built the Cornwall line.
Stone piers held viaducts of Memel pine.
Slender and frail they may have looked, but they
For half a century carried ore and clay,
Though later generations than my own
Have built my viaducts again in stone.
My piers still stand beside them sad and lone,
Gothic and picturesque and ivy-hung,
The sort of thing I liked to sketch when young.
Rich mineral Cornwall! All those tons of ore
Had to be shipped on reaching Saltash shore.
Redruth, St Austell, Camborne, Truro, Hayle
Could get no further by my iron rail.
Easy enough to bridge these shallow strands,
But how cross Tamar's swiftly running sands?
Deep in mid-stream I sunk a central pier
And slung from either bank what you see here:
Two hollow girders which I hoped would bring
Cornwall to Devon in an iron sling.

Enough of bridges, railways – on my dream
Of compassing the ocean with my steam.

At Bristol docks now full of weeds and silt
A new *Great Western* – for the sea I built
A paddle steamer whose enormous sides
Easily rode Atlantic waves and tides.
She reached New York but gained the second place –
Sirius of Liverpool had won the race.
At Bristol next I built them something new –
An iron steamship with propeller screw,
The biggest in the world, my famed *Great Britain*.
Bound for New York, the Irish coast she hit on
And lay off Antrim stranded, out of reach,
Like an old saucepan left on Brighton Beach.

The devil take them: I'm not beaten yet.
I'll build them something that they won't forget.
Paddle and screw combined and ironclad,
Take or leave her. Let them think me mad,
Into my drawings all my skill I hurled
To build the biggest steamship in the world.
London should have the contract. Millwall slips
Have seen the launching of our finest ships.
I'll build her here. D'you see her rising sides?
Look how the paddle o'er the houses rides.
See her propeller shaft, her narrow hull.
There are the damned financiers, greedy, dull,
That crook Scott Russell – but the working men,
They were my friends as always. With them then
I used to stand and smoke my time away,
Getting her ready for the launching day.
My ironclad, my fine *Great Eastern* see,
My co-creditors standing on the quay,
And looks of apprehension on them all.

She's off! She rides! Then fare you well, Millwall.
Never was such a floating palace seen,
Never were greater engines, nothing mean
About her fittings, and the grand saloon
Splendid enough to make the ladies swoon!
She's off! She rides! And I am leaving too,
Of Saltash bridge I took my final view.
Cornwall to Devon joined by rail at last,
The journey of my life was nearly past.
Too ill to move I lay upon my back
While Gooch's engine drew me down the track
Too ill to move. Dying at fifty-three,
This world means nothing. Now the world to be!
Such humbling thoughts upon a long last ride!

After Brunel got the news, he died
Broken like his *Great Eastern*, not to know
The swift repairs his ship would undergo.
How then with Gooch as captain she was able
To lay the first great transatlantic cable,
And after laying that lay many more
Like some great spider threaded shore to shore.
Never to know his fellow engineers
Would sling those chains between his Clifton piers,
Building Brunel's bridge to his memory.
This world means nothing. Now the world to be!

LA COMETA MORAIRA

How often on the terrace here
We sipped champagne instead of beer.
The gentle influence of the drink
Would turn us almond-blossom-pink.
The slightly stirring pines set free
An under-whisper from the sea.
Oh, may we often come again
To taste in Spain the dry champagne.

A LAMENT FOR MIDDLESEX

The sisters Progress and Destruction dwell
Where rural Middlesex once cast her spell.
Dear vanished county of such prosperous farms,
Where now are gone your weather-boarded charms?
Still in my dreams I see your sudden hills,
Your willowy brooks and winding lanes and rills,
The redbrick Georgian mansions' garden wall,
The little church, the spreading cedar tall.
See the Welsh Harp with undulating shore,
And hear beyond the road's arterial roar.
Your swinging signboards, barns with curly tiles,
Your little lakes, on which the sunset smiles.
Keats and Leigh Hunt in better lines than these
Have praised your misty fields and towering trees.
Constable's brush, with light and liquid fire,
Immortalised this unforgotten shire.
Dear Middlesex, dear vanished country friend,
Your neighbour, London, killed you in the end.

CASTLE HOWARD

Stay traveller! With no irreverent haste
Approach the mansion of a man of taste.
Hail, Castle Howard! Hail, Vanbrugh's noble dome
Where Yorkshire in her splendour rivals Rome!
Here the proud footman to the butler bows
But kisses Lucy when she milks the cows.

Here the proud butler on the steward waits
But shares his mistress at the castle gates.
Here fifty damsels list my lady's bells,
And a whole parish in one mansion dwells.
Chef, housekeeper, and humblest houseboy, all
In due gradation of the servants' hall,
Dependent on the slightest frown or smile
Of him who holds the Earldom of Carlisle.

But what are wealth and pomp of worldly state?
To yonder mausoleum soon or late,
Up those broad steps will go great Howard's dust –
A journey no man makes before he must.

LINES READ AT THE WING AIRPORT RESISTANCE MOVEMENT PROTEST MEETING, JUNE 1970

The birds are all killed and the flowers are all dead,
And the businessman's aeroplane booms overhead.
With chemical sprays we have poisoned the soil,
And the scent in our nostrils is diesel and oil.
The roads are all widened, the lanes are all straight,
So that rising executives won't have to wait.
For who'd use a footpath to Quainton or Brill
When a jet can convey him as far as Brazil?

SONNET

Now is my heart on fire, which once was chilled,
   Now are our bodies one which once were two,
   For you are part of me and I of you.
Of deep strong calm when turbulence is stilled,
In this sweet union which God has willed.
   Come closer, rest, I tremble through and through,
   All you can want of me I gladly do,
Now is the purpose of our lives fulfilled.

Is He not good, God who such rapture gives?
   Such overflowing ecstasy of joy.
     Touch, let me touch your warm enticing skin
That I may know my lover breathes and lives.
   My own, my darling sunkissed supple boy
     If this is sinful, what is wrong with sin?

REVENGE

A Mafia of motorbikes
Is waiting in his new machine.
He kicks the starter when he likes
And fills the world with noise obscene.

All Birmingham is in the air,
The pistons of his B.S.A.
Are detonating everywhere,
And this is what I hear him say:

'My mother was not nice to me
When I was young and weak and small.
The cruel din I'm setting free
Is my revenge upon you all.'

Shall we give Gibbs the go by?
   Great Gibbs of Aberdeen,
Who gave the town of Cambridge
   Its Senate House serene;
And every son of Oxford
   Can recognise he's home
When he sees upon the skyline
   The Radcliffe's mothering dome.
Placid above the chimney pots
   His sculptured steeples soar;
Windowless he designs his walls
   Above the traffic's roar.
Whenever you put stone on stone
   You edified the scene;
Your chaste baroque was on its own,
   Great Gibbs of Aberdeen.
A Tory and a Catholic,
   There's nothing quite so grand
As the baroque of your Chapel
   Of St Mary in the Strand.

MY LANDLADY'S DOG

Big and barking and smelly
  Is my landlady's horrible dog.
It has nipples all over its belly
  And its turds are the size of a log.
I know I must try to like it
  For it shows such affection to me,
And must never attempt to strike it
  If it thinks I'm the trunk of a tree.

GUYHIRN CHAPEL OF EASE

In brick and stone and glass and wood
   Three centuries has this beacon stood,
'Puritan relic of the past':
   Built to shine and built to last.
Long on its lone East Anglian level
   It praises God and shames the devil.

ST BARTHOLOMEW'S HOSPITAL

The ghost of Rahere still walks in Barts.
It gives an impulse to generous hearts,
It looks on pain with a pitying eye
And teaches us never to fear to die.

Eight hundred years of compassion and care
Have hallowed its fountain, stones and square.
Pray for us all as we near the Gate,
St Bart the Less and St Bart the Great.

WHO TOOK AWAY . . .

Who took away our counties
So rolling, wild and wide,
And called them after posh hotels,
Thamesdown and Humberside?

And where on earth is Avon?
Can it be holding yet
The lovely limestone church towers
Of what was Somerset?

LINES ON THE UNMASKING OF THE SURVEYOR OF THE QUEEN'S PICTURES

Poor old Bluntie! So they got him,
　'Mole Revealed' they say 'at last'.
On a bleak November morning,
　What an echo from the past!

Old Marlburian, I recall him,
　In his flannel bags and hat
Wandering by the River Talbot
　Sometimes straining at a gnat.

Who'd have guessed it – 'Blunt a traitor'
　And an homosexualist?
Carrying on with tar and waiter –
　There's a sight I'm glad I missed.

Now the nine-day wonder's over,
　Back he goes to Maida Vale.
In his comfy little Rover,
　Home to gin and ginger ale.

Was it worth it? Does it matter?
　In the end we do not know.
Now I'm madder than a hatter,
　Goodness me! It's time to go.

DAWLISH

Bird-watching colonels on the old sea wall,
Down here at Dawlish where the slow trains crawl:
Low tide lifting, on a shingle shore,
Long-sunk islands from the sea once more:
Red cliffs rising where the wet sands run,
Gulls reflecting in the sharp spring sun:
Pink-washed plaster by a sheltered patch,
Ilex shadows upon velvet thatch:
What interiors those panes suggest!
Queen of lodgings in the warm south-west. . . .

NOTES ON THE POEMS

EXPLANATORY NOTE

The following notes provide a date or approximate date of composition for each poem; for the previously published but uncollected poems, initial publication information is provided. Previously unpublished poems are so indicated, along with a note indicating the state and source of the poem (holograph manuscript, typed manuscript, archival repository), and whether the poem is signed or unsigned. Poems unrecorded in any published bibliography or other source are so noted. Some of the poems have additional commentary; this is generally restricted to explication of difficult allusions that help to pinpoint a poem's date of composition.

A.D. 1980. Published in *The Marlburian*, 5 March 1924. This was the official literary magazine of Marlborough College, which Betjeman attended from 1920 until 1925. Attributed by Bevis Hillier to Betjeman (*Young Betjeman*, p. 106) but not reprinted there. Though unsigned, it bears many of the hallmarks of later Betjeman verse, including mock-praise for the advancements of the present and future and name-dropping of products (in this instance, entirely invented). William Peterson urges caution in attributing it to Betjeman (*John Betjeman: A Bibliography*, p. 379); however, I concur with Hillier that it bears unmistakable Betjemanesque qualities.

Ye Olde Cottage (Quite Near a Town). Published in *The Heretick*, June 1924. Reprinted in Hillier, *Young Betjeman*, pp. 102–3. *The Heretick* was a newly founded school magazine at Marlborough College when Betjeman published this poem. Anthony Blunt was one of the magazine's founders; he recalled later that its editorial policy was 'to express our disapproval of the Establishment generally, of the more out-of-date and pedantic masters, of all forms of organized sport, of the Officers' Training Corps and of all . . . the intellectual discomforts of the school' (qtd. Hillier, *Young Betjeman*, p. 101). An essay by Blunt on the amorality of art caused school officials to shut down production of *The Heretick* (Hillier, p. 103). Only two issues were produced.

The Song of a Cold Wind. Published in *The Marlburian*, 23 October 1924; reprinted in *Public School Verse* 5 (1925), pp. 26–7. *Public School Verse* was an anthology published annually; one of its editors was the novelist Richard Hughes. There are a number of variants in the later publication; I use as my copy-text the original published in *The Marlburian*. An extract of this poem is printed in Hillier, *Young Betjeman*, pp. 106–7.

A Sentimental Poem. Published in *The Marlburian*, 18 December 1924. An extract of this poem is printed in Hillier, *Young Betjeman*, p. 107. Peterson urges caution in attributing it to Betjeman (Peterson, *John Betjeman*, p. 379), but I concur with Hillier's attribution owing to the poem's Betjemanesque qualities: references to Padstow and tamarisks, pools, and the colours green and silver recur with great frequency in Betjeman's poetry. A 'pisky' is the Cornish fairy or pixie.

Sweets and Cake. Written circa 1925–8. Previously unpublished. Title supplied by the editor. Untitled typescript with minor holograph revisions: Christ Church Archives, University of Oxford. As an undergraduate at Oxford, Betjeman wrote a number of scatological poems, most of them dealing with homosexual encounters between schoolboys, and these poems were assiduously collected by his friends. The fate of most of these poems is now unknown. This specimen is one of two that were in the possession of Tom Driberg, Baron Bradwell, and are among his papers deposited in the Christ Church Archives; a brief note in Driberg's hand indicates that Betjeman was the author. Both of the Driberg poems are catalogued by Peterson (*John Betjeman: A Bibliography*, pp. 417, 439); of the two poems, only 'Sweets and Cake' merits publication. Hillier, quoting the poem's final couplet, reports that Lionel Perry recited this poem when Betjeman visited him in 1979 (*Bonus*, p. 514), an indication of how deeply Betjeman's scatological wit impressed itself upon his closest friends.

Readers of *Summoned by Bells* will recall Betjeman's confession of same-sex crushes while an adolescent pupil at Marlborough College: 'First tremulous desires in Autumn stillness – / Grey eyes, lips laughing at another's joke, / A nose, a cowlick – a delightful illness / That put me off my food and off my stroke' (p. 72). In this poem, Betjeman is largely circumspect about the extent of his experiences but acknowledges one powerful relationship that changed his perspective on the horrors of daily life in a public school: 'Here was love / Too deep for words or touch. The golden downs / Looked over elm tops islanded in mist, / And short grass twinkled with blue butterflies. / Henceforward Marlborough shone' (pp. 73–4).

If in *Summoned by Bells* Betjeman dared not speak this love's name, the two poems in the Driberg papers at Christ Church fairly shout it out. Indeed, Betjeman provides here a comical antidote to the idealized portrait of adolescent male romantic friendship he offers in *Summoned by Bells*. In place of pastoral myth and innocent fantasy we encounter cheap, practical sex, while the haze of heartfelt emotion is reduced to awkward and self-centred desire. Though it may be pointless to read too much autobiographical confession into Betjeman's sexual poems, the temptation to do so may be strong, based on Hillier's report that one of the Marlborough classmates on whom Betjeman had a crush was a boy named Neville Greene (*Young Betjeman*, p. 115).

Is it possible that 'Sweets and Cake' and other poems in this vein were written to entertain his friends rather than to express desire or to recollect experience? They were certainly a product of Betjeman's time at Oxford, and Hillier notes that 'it is no exaggeration to say that the majority of John's undergraduate friends at Oxford were homosexual' (*Young Betjeman*, p. 178). In the essentially all-male world of school and university, Betjeman only gradually developed heterosexual tastes, and even in middle age, married and with a mistress, he often speculated about the percentage of homosexuality in himself and in other men (Hillier, *Bonus*, p. 66; Wilson, *Betjeman*, p. 67). Finding the trait of the 'sympathetic conversationalist' to be at the heart of Betjeman's character, A. N. Wilson cautions against making easy assumptions about Betjeman's sexuality: 'In the company of his many gay friends, he liked to play up the homosexual side of his nature, but there is no evidence of his ever having had a full-blown love affair with someone of his own sex though there might have been schoolboy or undergraduate fumblings' (*Betjeman*, p. 62).

Betjeman's sexual proclivities and activities are more complicated than Wilson indicates. A recently surfaced letter from Betjeman to his friend Lionel Perry, now deposited in the Magdalen College Archives, Oxford (MC:P323/C1/2), indicates that his sexual taste in adolescent masculinity lingered at least into his early adulthood and perhaps beyond. Though undated, textual evidence determines that this letter was written on Monday, 15 April 1929, when Betjeman was nearly 23 years old. After his rustication from Oxford in 1928, he completed one term as a schoolmaster and was then employed briefly as private secretary to Sir Horace Plunkett; after having been sacked by Plunkett, he stayed briefly with the Dugdales at Sezincote while waiting to start a new position as schoolmaster. It was at Sezincote that Betjeman entered into a relationship with an unidentified adolescent boy. In his account of this affair, he indicates to Perry that after some measures of seduction the boy was willing to proceed with sexual activity, and that only an effort of extreme willpower prevented him from taking that last step into forbidden acts. The handwritten letter is on Sezincote stationery:

Day after LORD'S DAY

My dear Lionel,
   I have got a job at £180 a year at a prep school in Barnet (20 minutes from Kings X) called Heddon

Court, Cockfoster's [*sic*], Herts. Barnet 2400. I go
there on the 22nd of this month & go to London on
Wednesday where I will stay for one night with E
[Ernest, his father] & the rest with the Dufferin's [*sic*] 9
Seamore Place Grosvenor 1289.

What I really wrote to tell you was that things have
gone well with the boy. My plan worked. He was all affec-
tion – dear thing & this morning he came in & insisted
on getting into bed with me – flung his arms round me,
stroked my hair pressed me very hard to him & kissed
me. Then ashamed, started to fight. Suddenly he stopp'd
as I held him powerless. Lay close up against me & said
'Do anything you like to me' THE LORD stepped in &
I remained chaste 'for as much as ye do it to one of these
little ones, ye do it TO ME –' oh Lionel – the boy – the
boy – the boy – oh Lionel – you smelly old thing.

tinkety tonk
J.B.

Not long after this, Betjeman entered into a series of
heterosexual romances, so it is impossible to draw easy
conclusions about his orientation(s). Whether as an
adult he acted upon his adolescent homosexual desire
is unknown, but that desire seems never entirely to
have left him. Later in life he revisited the fantasy of
sexual relations with adolescent males in a holograph
manuscript poem now in the Betjeman collection at the
University of Exeter (EUL MS 117/3/9). This manuscript
poem – undated, untitled, incomplete, and largely illeg-
ible – recounts how an exploration of a church led to an
unexpected sexual encounter with a choirboy.

160

Ultimately, the important critical perspective to be gained is not whether such poems are autobiographical confessions, but simply that Betjeman had a pronounced taste for the indecent, the scatological and comical expression of sexual experience. We may safely conclude that another poetic influence heretofore unrecognized was the Earl of Rochester.

Dentist's Dining Room. Written circa 1925–8. Previously unpublished. Unsigned typescript: John Murray Archives. A handwritten note at the bottom of the typescript indicates that it was written when Betjeman was an undergraduate at Oxford. The typescript itself appears to be part of a letter sent from the Beresford Hotel, Birchington-on-Sea, Kent, where Betjeman was staying with his employer, Sir Horace Plunkett, in February 1929. Preceding the poem on the slightly torn letter are these typed sentences: 'I'm here for a week – a "bungalow hotel" in the Japanese s[tyle] affected by Anglo-Indian Colonel's wives. 1 minute from the [sea] and a nice big ball-room.' Following the poem is the single typed sentence, 'Hope you have recovered from your 'flu.' Pencilled at the bottom in handwriting that appears to be Betjeman's are two phrases: 'Mark Ogilvie Grant' and 'as undergraduate'.

Are there additional clues that help to date the poem? On 10 February Betjeman wrote to Patrick Balfour from the Beresford Hotel with a similar description: '[It] is furnished in that Japanese style so popular with the wives of Anglo-Indian Colonels who retire to Camberley. There is a ballroom and an "Oak and Pewter" room which is very pretty' (*Letters, Volume One: 1926–1951*, p. 52). A few days later Betjeman returned to Surrey with Plunkett, where he wrote to Mary St Clair-Erskine. She was recovering from influenza, as apparently was their mutual friend Mark Ogilvie-Grant. Betjeman concludes, 'I will send you my poems when I have typed out some copies of them. Mark has had 'flu' (*Ibid.*, p. 53). My sense is that if Betjeman was sending copies of his poems to Mary St Clair-Erskine, he also likely sent at least one poem – 'Dentist's Dining Room' – to Mark Ogilvie-Grant in early February 1929.

Clearly the poem was written no later than 1929, but ultimately we have only the pencilled notation 'as undergraduate' to pinpoint the period of composition. At some point years later, Ogilvie-Grant must have returned the letter and poem to Betjeman, who then mentioned it to his publisher, Jock Murray. Apparently Murray had asked for a copy of this poem so that it could be considered for publication in Betjeman's next collection. Betjeman's secretary, the Revd Harold Farrington, located the poem and sent it on to Murray with a note, dated 31 July 1961: 'I remember you asking about the enclosed poem some time ago. I knew it was somewhere in the flat, and in the course of a grand cleaning up to-day I found it' (John Murray Archives).

The London furniture behemoth Drage's rose to prominence in the early 1920s with its mass-market appeal; the 'Drage Way' for financing furniture beyond one's means was launched in 1922 in their 'Mr Everyman' campaign. Before long, 'Drage Way' was adopted as a general advertising slogan rather than merely a financing plan and was so well known that by 1925 it was parodied in a music-hall song. By the early 1930s, Drage's would be considered down-market; by the mid-1930s the company was in financial and social decline, and it was liquidated in 1937. 'Drage-way' furniture also appears in Betjeman's poem

'The Outer Suburbs' (1931); and in *Keep the Aspidistra Flying*, George Orwell's protagonist writes a satirical poem about the lives of middle-class people struggling to make instalment payments on Drage's furniture.

Throwley Forstal is a hamlet in Kent, five or six miles southwest of Faversham.

Sezincote. Written circa 1926–30. Previously unpublished. Title supplied by the editor. Untitled typescript and holograph manuscript: John Murray Archives. Sezincote, a country house near Moreton-in-Marsh, was at the time of writing owned by Colonel Arthur Dugdale and his wife, Ethel. It was built in the Indian style in 1805 by Sir Charles Cockerell, sold to James Dugdale in 1884, and then to Sir Cyril Kleinwort in 1944. The house is now in the care of Sir Cyril's grandson, Edward Peake. (The Rushouts were descendants of Sir Charles Cockrell: having inherited the Rushout Baronetcy through his maternal grandfather, Sir Charles's son and heir adopted the Rushout name in lieu of his patronymic.) The poem imagines Sezincote's various architectural features and works of art joining voices in thanks to Colonel Dugdale for preserving the house from ruin and enjoining him to repair and restore its famed orangery. That did not occur until the 1950s, when the Kleinwort family engaged in substantial restoration work on Sezincote and saved it from certain ruin.

Having met John Dugdale at Oxford, Betjeman became a frequent guest at Sezincote throughout his undergraduate days and even in the years following his rustication. 'Stately and strange it stood, the Nabob's house, / Indian without and coolest Greek within': so he described it in *Summoned by Bells*, with its domes and minarets rising mysteriously in the Cotswold hills (p. 99). Betjeman also recalled the social education he received from the Dugdales: 'First steps in learning how to be a guest, / First wood-smoke-scented luxury of life / In the large ambience of a country house' (p. 98). Sezincote became a 'second home' to Betjeman (p. 100). When he published *Mount Zion* in 1931, he dedicated it to Ethel Dugdale; a half-page woodcut engraving of Sezincote is followed by this tribute: 'Constantly under those minarets I have been raised from the deepest depression and spent the happiest days of my life' (p. 5).

Pastoral Incident. Written circa 1927–9. Previously unpublished. Signed typescript: McPherson Library Special Collections, University of Victoria. The typescript, one surviving copy of which is dated 1929, was given by Betjeman to a friend who unearthed it and returned it to him in the 1970s (Peterson, *John Betjeman*, p. 447). The poem illustrates Betjeman's capacity to hold simultaneously both serious and playful views of a subject. Here in the manner of Alexander Pope, Betjeman treats the Dugdales in mock-heroic fashion as Arthur saves Ethel from a loathsome insect. Betjeman's references to British newspapers allude to the strongly divided politics in the Dugdale household; as Betjeman recalled in *Summoned by Bells*, 'She and her son and we were on the Left, / But Colonel Dugdale was Conservative.' Nevertheless, there was a 'love between those seeming opposites' (p. 100).

A Squib on Norman Cameron. Written circa 1927. Previously unpublished. Title supplied by the editor.

Untitled, signed holograph manuscript: New York Public Library, Berg Collection. Norman Cameron (1905–53) was a Scottish poet whom Betjeman had known when they worked together on Oxford's student newspaper, *The Cherwell*. In a piece entitled 'The Boar's Hill Scheme' in the 18 June 1927 issue of the paper, satirizing the taste for Arts and Crafts, Betjeman mocked Cameron as a 'rising craftsman' who 'has designed some picturesque cottages with bizarre gardens dedicated to Truth' (p. 199).

The source of the squib, whether anger or jealousy or some other motive, is unknown. The accusation of 'concentrated pride' is, I would venture, a misunderstanding on Betjeman's part; one of Cameron's biographers refers to his 'lifelong talent for friendship' and notes a dominant character trait as 'self-derision' (Helena Nelson, 'Norman Cameron [1905–1953]', in Jay Parini, ed., *British Writers: Supplement IX* [New York: Scribner's, 2004], pp. 17–32), which hardly seems consonant with Betjeman's perception of self-puffery on Cameron's part. In any case, Betjeman's antipathy must have been short-lived as Cameron was among many old friends from the *Cherwell* he invited to write for the *Architectural Review* in the early 1930s (Hillier, *Young Betjeman*, pp. 271–2). Like the Restoration-era satires echoed in Betjeman's squib, it seems probable that this manuscript circulated among mutual acquaintances, for Cameron was aware that Betjeman had called him 'puffed up'; however, there appears to have been no lingering animosity on Cameron's part, as the following holograph letter from Cameron to Betjeman suggests (archived in the University of Victoria McPherson Library Special Collections and never before published):

49ᶜ British Grove
Chiswick, W.4.
29/11/35

Dear Betjeman,

I left your letter at Len's address, which is 18 Black Lion Lane, Hammersmith, W.6.

How did you get that notion of me being a gloomy despiser? I remember that at Oxford you accused me of being 'puffed up'. My face must belie me – I'm not that sort of chap at all, as Len could tell you. Len was saying a day or two ago that we should meet for lunch some time, and I was looking forward to it.

I'm glad you like my poems, and I agree with your remarks about Dylan Thomas and Boldero. But you've got that wrong about a coterie. Dylan has to go about seeing a lot of literary blokes, because his only source of income is from poems and reviews, but I seldom see any of such people. Certainly neither Dylan nor I feel any coterie – kinship with anyone else.

Len is very grateful to you. He says you've been a great help to him in dealing with Shell over this film he's been making for them.

Let me know through Len if you'd care to meet anywhere for a meal.

Yours
Norman Cameron

'Len' is Len Lye (1901–80), a New Zealand-born experimental documentary filmmaker, kinetic sculptor and avant-garde artist. An innovator in the new medium of colour film, Lye drew the attention of Shell-Mex, whose film unit had been created in 1934 by Jack Beddington, for whom Betjeman was also working, to produce prestige advertisements. The film that Cameron credits Betjeman for assisting Lye with is, most likely, *The Birth of the Robot* (1936). Produced in 'Gasparcolor' and using a soundtrack extracted from Gustav Holst's *The Planets*, this animated film is a puppet fantasy advertising Shell lubrication oils. 'Boldero' was a pen name of Geoffrey Grigson, who founded (and edited) *New Verse*, the leading poetry journal of the 1930s. Cameron was a major contributor to *New Verse*, though Betjeman himself never found favour with Grigson (Hillier, *Young Betjeman*, p. 358).

Blisland, Bodmin. Published in *Oxford Outlook*, June 1927. Two typescript drafts are deposited in the Poetry Collection, The State University of New York at Buffalo; along with some minor variants, those drafts are missing the final two stanzas as published in *Oxford Outlook*. Betjeman published this poem under the pseudonym 'Dorothie Harbinger'. He had a propensity to publish under *noms de plume* throughout his youth (cf. Hillier, *Young Betjeman*, pp. 102–9). In addition to publishing in *Oxford Outlook*, he also co-edited at least one issue with John Sparrow; other editors in the 1920s were Graham Greene and Isaiah Berlin.

Home Thoughts from Exile. Published in *The Cherwell*, 17 March 1928, p. 201. Hillier printed an extract of this poem in *Young Betjeman*, p. 186. Betjeman was a regular contributor to the Oxford undergraduate newspaper, *The Cherwell*, and was later its editor. It had a strong literary bent throughout the 1920s. The reference to 'St Ernest's Hall' is Betjeman's reflection on the increasingly tense and difficult relationship with his father, Ernest Betjemann.

Work. Written circa 1927–32. Previously unpublished and unrecorded. Unsigned typescript: The Poetry Collection, The State University of New York at Buffalo. Liberty's department store encouraged English designers in the Arts and Crafts movement, stocked and sold their wares, and became closely associated with the design. Betjeman satirized Arts and Crafts regularly in the Oxford paper, *The Cherwell*, but after a few years at the *Architectural Review* (1930–5) he softened his perspective.

Popular Song. Written circa 1927–32. Previously unpublished. Unsigned typescript: The Poetry Collection, The State University of New York at Buffalo. More than twenty years before Nancy Mitford and Professor Alan Ross ignited a firestorm of interest in 'U and non-U' English usage, and more than twenty years before his own satiric contribution in 'How to Get on in Society', Betjeman satirized middle-class speech acts and shopping habits in this poem. Bon Marché was a large and popular department store in Brixton, South London. A.B.C. (Aerated Bread Company) was a chain of self-service tea shops designed especially for Victorian women to eat publicly without a male escort; by the 1920s, there were more than 250 A.B.C. tea shops in London. Betjeman probably was appalled by the packaged and tinned artifice of the food as well as by the self-service nature of the establishments. Lines from this poem appear in the script of his BBC radio broadcast, 'One Hour of Modern Variety' (23 January 1933).

Nine O'Clock. Written circa 1927–32. Previously unpublished. Unsigned typescript: The Poetry Collection, The State University of New York at Buffalo. The Wharncliffe Rooms served as the Hotel Great Central's ballroom. Here Betjeman continues with the satirical vein of middle-class satire established in 'Work' and 'Popular Song'.

Emily Wren. Written circa 1927–32. Previously unpublished. Unsigned typescript: The Poetry Collection, The State University of New York at Buffalo.

The Tamarisks. Written circa 1927–32. Previously unpublished. Unsigned typescript: The Poetry Collection, The State University of New York at Buffalo. The tamarisk (or tamarix) is native to desert climates but was sometimes used as hedges in Cornwall, which in Betjeman's youth attracted the British middle classes for its nearly tropical seaside climate.

Sonnet. Written circa 1927–32. Previously unpublished. Unsigned typescript: The Poetry Collection, The State University of New York at Buffalo. This is the first of several poems that present a unique and seldom-heard voice of Betjeman's. Here the young poet seems to be working in the vein of Shelley: depressive in tone, complex in syntax, as if to be a poet one must be a Romantic.

Wisteria Branches. Written circa 1927–32. Previously unpublished. Title supplied by the editor. Untitled and unsigned typescript: The Poetry Collection, The State University of New York at Buffalo. Another poem in which the young poet, experimenting with Romanticism, attempts to find his voice and vision.

A Poem by My Old Bear Archibald. Written circa 1927–32. Previously unpublished. Unsigned typescripts: The Poetry Collection, The State University of New York at Buffalo; McPherson Library Special Collections, University of Victoria. As in the poem 'Archibald' in *Collected Poems*, Betjeman sustains the sense of gloom and despair emanating from Archie. For all the solace Betjeman found in his actual teddy bear, as a literary character Archie seems terribly remote, judgemental and uncomforting. Perhaps because this poem is not merely about Archie but is spoken by him, it is strange and alienating, with many unidentified allusions. Why does Archie imagine Gladstone in a spun cocoon? Why does he worry about a killing bottle, and why do the winds cry out 'Endeavour'? Answers to these questions elude me still, though that may well be the point; Bevis Hillier suggests that this piece may be Betjeman's 'attempt at a sheer nonsense poem' (correspondence with the author, 26 July 2018).

Harvest Bells. Written circa 1927–32. Previously unpublished. Unsigned typescript: The Poetry Collection, The State University of New York at Buffalo. St Lawrence Church, Bourton-on-the-Hill, has striking views to the south toward Sezincote, only a mile or so away. Its ring of six bells is one of the most impressive in the region; the three oldest bells date to 1677, two of them to 1792, and the most recent to 1873. Betjeman would have easily heard its peal on his many visits with the Dugdales at Sezincote.

Country Silence. Written circa 1928. Previously unpublished. Typescript: The Poetry Collection, The State University of New York at Buffalo. A holograph fair copy of this poem is deposited in the Beinecke Rare Book and Manuscript Library, Yale University, with the title 'Quaker Silence' (possibly Betjeman's original title). The Yale manuscript contains several interesting variants, including the following substitutions: 'one' for 'rest' (ll. 4, 22), 'footsteps' for 'horse hoofs' (l. 7), 'noise' for 'sound' (l. 11), and 'chirrup' for 'scratching' (l. 13). A third version of this poem, a signed typescript, is deposited in the archives of Magdalen College, Oxford; it is titled 'Written in a Garden' and is missing lines 7–8 (MS P323/C1/25). Bevis Hillier made a transcription of a handwritten draft of this poem, which he kindly sent to me some years ago; his transcription includes the following signature: 'J. Betjeman, Thorpe House School, Oval Way, Gerrard's Cross, Bucks.' Since Betjeman was a master at Thorpe House School for one term in the spring of 1928, this would indicate the likeliest date of composition to be 1928. However, this signature appears on neither the Buffalo typescript nor the Yale holograph manuscript, so I have not been able to verify it. A much condensed and revised version of the poem was published in *Oxford, China and Italy*, ed. Edward Chaney and Neil Ritchie (London: Thames and Hudson, 1984), p. 13, under the title 'Lines written in the Twenties in the garden of the Spread Eagle at Thame, a hostelry frequented at the time by Harold Acton'. This book is a collection of tributes to Acton.

Channel Crossing. Written circa 1928–9. Previously unpublished. Title supplied by the editor. Untitled and unsigned typescript: The Poetry Collection, The State University of New York at Buffalo. A four-line fragment on this same typescript is dated 5 August 1929. In 1810 Lord Byron recreated Leander's mythical swim across the Dardanelles. On 7 October 1927 Mercedes Gleitze became the first British woman to swim the English Channel and on 5 April 1928 was the first person, man or woman, to swim the Strait of Gibraltar. This extraordinarily clever poem reveals Betjeman's early interest in Romanticism yet rejects its powerful pull in an impressive show of independence. He opts for a trochaic metre (which would become one of his signature rhythms) and identifies not with the myth (as Byron did) but with the modern swimmer. In replicating Leander's fabled swim, Byron engaged in 'poetic emulation'; in contrast, by swimming in her own way and place Gleitze stepped out of the shadows of her forebears. As Gleitze swam, so must Betjeman write: in his own way and place. This is a rejection of 'poetic emulation'.

Eighteenth-Century Print. Written circa 1929–30. Previously unpublished. Unsigned typescript: Beinecke Rare Book and Manuscript Library, Yale University. The American bibliophile Duncan Andrews was perhaps the first to make a systematic effort to collect Betjeman's works, and after meeting Betjeman in 1963 he made his first purchase of manuscripts. This unpublished poem – for Betjeman highly unusual in syntax and metre – was part of Andrews' Betjeman collection. The actual picture – assuming it was not imagined – has not been identified. The poem is difficult to date, but its formal properties offer a clue. As a young poet struggling to find his unique voice, Betjeman often experimented with modernist techniques. This poem rhymes and scans, so it is not free verse; however, it is free of a formal pattern, which is something he practised in the late 1920s through the early 1930s, *viz.* 'For Nineteenth-Century Burials' in *Mount Zion*, or 'City', 'Clash Went the Billiard Balls' and 'Exchange of Livings' in *Continual Dew*.

Lerici 1930. Written circa 1930. Previously unpublished. Title supplied by the editor. Untitled and unsigned typescript: The Poetry Collection, The State University of New York at Buffalo. Poem signed 'Lerici, Oct. 1930', but there is no concrete evidence that the poem was composed in 1930, nor is Betjeman known to have travelled to the Italian Riviera. As a student at Marlborough College, Betjeman had the reputation of a budding poet given to an earnest manner and an ornate, even florid style, so despite the date of 1930 it may have been written as early as 1924 or 1925, when his first poems were appearing in the school magazine, the *Marlburian*. Whenever it was written, this ode demonstrates the lingering influence of the Romantics – in this instance, Percy Shelley, who drowned at Lerici in 1822 – on Betjeman's developing poetic imagination. It has a highly original stanzaic pattern and rhyme scheme.

Evangelical Hymn. Written circa 1929–32. Previously unpublished. Title supplied by the editor. Untitled holograph manuscript: McPherson Library Special Collections, University of Victoria. Both the handwriting and the tone date this poem to the period when Betjeman was composing the poems that would find their way into *Mount Zion*.

Sudden Conversion. Written circa 1929–32. Previously unpublished and unrecorded. Holograph manuscript: Harry Ransom Center, University of Texas. Fair copy with minor revisions in a notebook that contains poems published in *Mount Zion* and *Continual Dew*. That one of those poems ('Dorset') was first published as early as 1932 gives a strong indication that the poems in this notebook were written no later than 1932. The subject of evangelical non-conformity suggests that this poem may have been considered for inclusion in *Mount Zion*. Wincarnis is a tonic wine, at one time fortified with a meat extract – hence its name.

Zion. Written circa 1929. Published in 1931 under the title 'Competition' with several variants in *Mount Zion* but excluded from *Collected Poems* by Lord Birkenhead. Auden saw its value and included the poem in the collection of Betjeman's prose and poetry that he edited for an American audience, *Slick but Not Streamlined* (1947). My copy text is the typescript in the Poetry Collection, The State University of New York at Buffalo, MS B43F19. It was written as early as 1929, perhaps earlier. On the verso of the Buffalo typescript is a sketch Betjeman made of the dustjacket he had in mind for his first book of poetry; it was to be titled *Chapel and Spa* and was to be published by Philip Sainsbury in 1929. The current printing restores Betjeman's original title and his original concluding four lines; here are the final four lines as published in *Mount Zion*:

> Short lived! Short lived! in this world of ours
> Are Triumph and Praise and Prayer.
> What of Mount Carmel Baptists (Strict),
> For they've central heating there?

The only other significant variant is that the word 'rock' is substituted for 'split' in the third line of the final stanza: 'Your traceried windows may rock with song.' Peterson records this poem under both titles (N93 and N676).

The Outer Suburbs. Published in 1931 in *Mount Zion* but excluded from *Collected Poems* by Lord Birkenhead. A typescript draft of this poem in the Poetry Collection, The State University of New York at Buffalo, bears the earlier title 'North London', and the final line reads 'Elizabethan, overhead'. See notes to 'Dentist's Dining Room' for an explanation of the significance of a 'Drage-way drawing room'. Peterson records this poem under both titles (N399 and N451).

St Aloysius Church, Oxford. Published in 1931 in *Mount Zion* but excluded from *Collected Poems* by Lord Birkenhead. St Aloysius is the Roman Catholic parish church in central Oxford, also known as the Oxford Observatory. Built in 1875, its formal name is the Oxford Oratory Church of St Aloysius Gonzaga. When the poem was published in *Mount Zion*, Betjeman added a clarifying footnote on the implied meaning of the word 'Reality' in the final line: 'In its mystical sense.'

Charterhouse School Song. Written in 1931. Previously unpublished. Title supplied by the editor. Holograph manuscript: The Poetry Collection, The State University of New York at Buffalo. Poem written on the verso of a communication from estate agents Saunders & Golmick, dated 28 May 1931.

London Spreading. Published unsigned and untitled in *The Architectural Review*, November 1931, to accompany a reproduction of three paintings by Algernon Newton. The paintings are of suburban London houses in Hampstead Garden Suburb, along the Regent's Canal, and in Bayswater. Title supplied by the editor. Identified as a genuine Betjeman composition by Bevis Hillier, who quotes an extract (*Young Betjeman*, pp. 272–3).

Satires of Circumstance. In an Oxford Lodging. Written circa 1931–2. Previously unpublished. Holograph manuscript with revisions: The Poetry Collection, The State University of New York at Buffalo. Signed 'T.H.'. Thomas Hardy published a series of poems called *Satires of Circumstance* (1914). Betjeman writes in Hardy's vein: the subject, the treatment and the structure of the poem are all Hardyesque. This manuscript is titled 'A Satire of Circumstance' and subtitled 'In an Oxford Lodging'. I have paired this poem with 'At Tea' and given them the group title of 'Satires of Circumstance'. For the poem's final line, Betjeman considered then rejected this: 'For little he thought that his wife would call.'

Satires of Circumstance. At Tea. Written circa 1931–2. Previously unpublished and unrecorded. Title supplied by the editor. Untitled holograph manuscript with revisions: The Poetry Collection, The State University of New York at Buffalo. Although untitled, it bears many stylistic and formal similarities with Hardy's *Satires of Circumstance* and with Betjeman's intentional imitation of Hardy, 'In an Oxford Lodging', so I have paired them together under the general title of 'Satires of Circumstance'. Two lines rejected and revised by Betjeman reveal the poem's subject had suffered an additional loss: 'But as she was unmarried . . . who is it who knocks / At her mind's locked door, but he who forsook her.'

The Heartless Heart's Ease: A Lament by Tom Moore. Written in 1932. Previously unpublished. Holograph manuscript: The Poetry Collection, The State University of New York at Buffalo. This is the 'lost poem' referred to in a footnote in Betjeman's *Letters: Volume 2, 1951–1984*, p. 577. Betjeman wrote the poem for Lady Pansy Lamb (1904–99), daughter of the fifth Earl of Longford, wife of the Australian painter (and former physician) Henry Lamb, and an author under her maiden name, Pansy Pakenham. Betjeman playfully exaggerates the married Pansy's 'heartless' rejection of him as well as his own crush on her and his status as an outsider. He was a regular guest of the Lambs in their home in Coombe Bissett, Wiltshire, along with such figures as Bryan Guinness, L. P. Hartley and Lord David Cecil. Thomas Moore (1779–1852), whose taste for anapestic metre the poem appropriates, was an Irish poet of whom Betjeman was rather fond.

The Most Popular Girl in the School. Written in 1932. Previously unpublished. Recited on BBC radio on 23 January 1933. Holograph manuscript: Harry Ransom Center, University of Texas. Two stanzas were published by producer Lance Sieveking, who provides fascinating background on this and other early Betjeman radio broadcasts, in *John Betjeman and Dorset* (Dorset Natural History and Archaeological Society, 1963). For more background on this broadcast, see Hillier, *New Fame*, pp. 147–9. In the radio broadcast, Betjeman adopts the persona of 'the Highbrow of the Upper Fifth' and attributes the poem's authorship to his imaginary sister, Miss Jessie Betjeman. In the surviving broadcast script, Betjeman's poem recitation is followed by a 'Female Voice' reciting lines from Betjeman's 'Popular Song', also first published in the present volume.

The Electrification of Lambourne End. Published unsigned in *The Architectural Review*, November 1933, and subtitled 'A Poem in the Manner of the Rev. George Crabbe'. It opens with an 'Apology': 'The poem, which starts in the next column and goes on for such a long time in the others, must not be taken as a declamation against the benefits of electricity. It serves to show the old-fashioned abuses of electricity. Within the last ten years electricity has made such vast strides that the old shams of mediæval electric lanterns, mediæval electric log fires, [and] mediæval electrically lit beams have passed away. This is an old-fashioned poem on an old-fashioned theme. Antiquarians will appreciate it as such; those who see in electricity a new and beautiful life and landscape for England will understand its salutary message.'

Edgware. Published untitled in the *Evening Standard*, 25 April 1934, as part of an article by Betjeman headlined ' "I'm No Anna," Says Mae West'. Title supplied by the editor from the joking attribution that follows the poem: 'So wrote, or would have written, the poet Longfellow about Edgware.' Transcription kindly provided by Dr Anne Mouron, Bodleian Library, Oxford. The poem gently satirizes the transformation of a palatial eighteenth-century estate into a modern suburb. Bevis Hillier discusses and reprints two poems written in a similar vein and published about the same time in the *Evening Standard* (*New Fame*, pp. 51–2). Lord Beaverbrook had appointed Betjeman film critic of the *Evening Standard* in 1933.

The Wykehamist at Home. Published in May 1934 in *New Oxford Outlook* and again in July 1934 in *Review of Reviews*. It was included in *Continual Dew* in 1937 but excluded from *Collected Poems* by Lord Birkenhead. Former pupils of Winchester College are known as Old Wykehamists after the school's founder, William of Wykeham, who also founded New College, Oxford.

Tea with the Poets. Published in 1937 in *Continual Dew* but excluded from *Collected Poems* by Lord Birkenhead. 'Primula Guest' was Betjeman's pseudonym for 'a smashing Berkshire girl called "Ursula West"' (qtd. Peterson, *John Betjeman*, p. 25). In an early holograph manuscript, Betjeman had substituted 'Wystan Auden' for 'C. Day Lewis', 'Mrs Pudney' for 'Mr Grogley', and 'Ursula Guest' for 'Primula Guest'.

A Poet's Prayer. Written circa 1937. Previously unpublished. Title supplied by the editor. Untitled holograph manuscript: McPherson Library Special Collections, University of Victoria. The poem is nearly impossible to date with certainty. However, its serious spiritual content, together with the handwriting, suggest the likelihood of composition around 1937, when Betjeman read the Revd Francis Harton's *Elements of the Spiritual Life* (London: SPCK, 1932) and attempted to transform his life according to the spiritual principles laid out by Father Harton, the Vicar of Baulking.

On Miss E. Badger, 9 Beverley Gardens, Wembley Park, Middlesex, Who Sat Opposite to Me on the GWR, Ascension Day 1939. Written circa 1939. Previously unpublished. Holograph manuscript: Beinecke Rare Book and Manuscript Library, Yale University. The specificity of the title suggests an immediacy of composition rather than a recollection in tranquillity. Nevertheless, the poem's dark themes possibly inspired later Betjeman poems such as 'Late-Flowering Lust', the earliest draft of which is dated 1948 (Peterson, *John Betjeman*, p. 430).

Big Business. Written circa 1939–40. Previously unpublished. Typescript: McPherson Library Special Collections, University of Victoria. Holograph manuscript: The Poetry Collection, The State University of New York at Buffalo. The manuscript at Buffalo bears Betjeman's original title, 'Premier De Luxe Brochure', but the typescript at Victoria is titled 'Big Business'. The poem expresses Betjeman's hostility to the world of business, perhaps recalling or imagining callous business practices at his father's cabinet-makers firm, G. Betjemann & Sons. There is little to date precisely the poem's composition, though it appears to have been typed on the same typewriter as an early draft of 'Sunday Afternoon Service in St Enodoc Church, Cornwall', first published in 1944 (The Poetry Collection, The State University of New York at Buffalo MS B42F4). Betjeman's interest in the dramatic monologue first appears about this time; his earliest dramatic monologues, 'In Westminster Abbey' and 'Bristol and Clifton', were published in 1939 and 1940 respectively.

Chestnut Hair. Written circa 1940–1. Previously unpublished. Multiple holograph manuscripts: McPherson

Library Special Collections, University of Victoria. Beyond a handwriting analysis, there is little to offer concrete evidence of a date of composition for this poem. The most powerful clue is in one of the preliminary drafts, where instead of 'the smell of stew' Betjeman tried out the phrase, 'the blackout stink'. This would point to the period of the Blitz as the setting of the poem, though the composition might have occurred later. The poem's form – a sonnet – may offer another clue. Betjeman wrote very few sonnets in his life, but in the early and mid-1940s he wrote and published four: 'Lake District' (1940), 'On an Old-Fashioned Water-Colour of Oxford' (1943), 'The Planster's Vision' (1945) and 'To Uffington Ringers' (1946). He also wrote several sonnets in the 1970s – 'On a Painting by Julius Olsson R.A.' (1971), 'Shetland 1973' (not published until 1982), and five sonnets for Robin Maugham's novel *The Barrier* (1973) – but the steady handwriting of the 'Chestnut Hair' manuscripts definitively dates this piece to well before the 1970s. Two internal features may point to its period of composition. 'Dismal Desmond' – a droopy Dalmatian dog, almost as depressive in appearance as Eeyore – was a highly popular stuffed animal before World War II. Desmond was introduced in 1926 and was in production until 1935 or 1936. The 'Good Luck Calendar' I have not been able to identify definitively, but it was probably something produced by the highly successful Raphael Tuck & Sons company.

Clifton 1940. Written in 1940. Previously unpublished and unrecorded. Title supplied by the editor. Unsigned typescript: McPherson Library Special Collections, University of Victoria. Typescript titled, inexplicably, 'Portrait of the

Artist as a Young Can', and signed 'Clifton. April 1940.' When the war broke out, Betjeman applied to the R.A.F. but was turned down and was instead assigned to the films division of the Ministry of Information, in which capacity he visited Bristol and Clifton in 1940. The Victoria and the Mauretania are pubs in Clifton; the Grand most likely refers to the popular ballroom at Clifton's Grand Spa Hotel.

Order Reigns in Warsaw. Written circa 1941–2 when Betjeman was working as press attaché to the British Embassy in Dublin and recited at an arts event hosted by the Polish General Consul to Ireland in January 1942. Published posthumously in *The Observer*, 29 April 1990, p. 3, and in *The Betjemanian* 2 (1990), pp. 34–5. For more details, see Horace Liberty, 'The Background to the Betjeman Poem "Order Reigns in Warsaw"', *The Betjemanian* 28 (2017), pp. 28–30.

Prologue Specially Written for the 70th Anniversary Gaiety Theatre, Dublin. Written in 1941. Printed as a broadside inserted loose into a souvenir history of the Gaiety Theatre, Dublin; the prologue preceded a performance of Shaw's *Caesar and Cleopatra*. Brief excerpts were published in Hillier, *New Fame*, p. 215, and Lycett Green, ed., *Letters, Volume One: 1926–1951*, p. 272.

To Uffington Ringers. Written in 1942 and considered for inclusion in *New Bats for Old Belfries*. Published in 1946 in *Diversion*, ed. Hester W. Chapman and Princess Romanovsky-Pavlovsky, for the benefit of the Yugoslav Relief Society. For more details, see Peterson, *John Betjeman*, p. 462.

Rosemary Hall. Written circa 1943. Published posthumously in *The Betjemanian* 14 (2003), p. 27. Betjeman wrote the poem after meeting Emily, Lady Hemphill (later Emily Villiers-Stuart), in Ireland during the war. Emily, an American by birth and the wife of the fourth Baron Hemphill, was also the inspiration for 'Ireland with Emily' (1944). In this poem he imagines her in school in New England. For more details on Betjeman's relations with Emily Villiers-Stuart, see Hillier, *New Fame*, pp. 227–9.

The Tailwaggers' Friend. Written circa 1945. Previously unpublished. Title supplied by the editor. Untitled holograph manuscript: Beinecke Rare Book and Manuscript Library, Yale University. This poem is about the dogs belonging to 'Colonel' George Kolkhorst, an Oxford don. On the manuscript Betjeman made sketches of the four dogs at the top; in the background is a sketch of Yarnton Manor, home of Colonel Kolkhorst, and at the bottom a caricature of Kolkhorst himself. Betjeman stayed with Kolkhorst at Yarnton throughout the summer of 1945. He nurtured a lifelong dislike of dogs and wrote in *Summoned by Bells* that Kolkhorst's rooms in Oxford 'smelled of mice and chicken soup and dogs' (p. 96). An unfinished holograph draft of a poem titled 'Yarnton School Song' includes the following lines: 'Some have died & some have departed / Quarrelled with Toby or kicked the dogs' (McPherson Library Special Collections, University of Victoria, John Betjeman Collection MS PTO 068). See also 'My Landlady's Dog' and note.

Margate, 1946. Written in 1946. Previously unpublished and unrecorded. Typescript with minor holograph revisions: McPherson Library Special Collections, University of Victoria. In 1940 Betjeman wrote and published in *The Listener* a poem titled 'Margate, 1940' (published again in 1945 in *New Bats in Old Belfries*), which celebrates the simple pleasures of life beside the seashore as the shadows of war darken over England; it concludes with the elegiac couplet, 'And I think, as the fairy-lit sights I recall, / It is those we are fighting for, foremost of all.' In 1946 Betjeman made a return visit to Margate to witness the war damage and see what life was returning. The ringing church bells make this poem a prayer of thanksgiving for deliverance.

A Memory of 1940. Written in 1946 and published post-humously in *The Betjemanian* 7 (1995), pp. 8–9. The poem reflects the dim view Betjeman took of Clement Attlee's socialist politics, and in A. N. Wilson's opinion the poem 'was considered too hostile to the great British worker to be publishable in Attlee's Britain' (Wilson, *Betjeman*, p. 159). There is no evidence the poem was offered to any magazine. It must have been lost when *A Few Late Chrysanthemums* was being compiled in 1954, but it resurfaced in 1966 and was considered for *High and Low*. By then, its satiric targets were twenty years old, and both Birkenhead and Murray persuaded Betjeman not to include it. Birkenhead wrote to Murray in April 1966, 'It belongs, after all, to a bygone era of rationing and shortages and might seem out of place now. It is a pity because I think it is one of the funniest he ever wrote . . . A whole generation has arisen which would not know what "basic" meant' (qtd. Hillier, *Bonus*, p. 238). 'Basic' is slang for wartime petrol rations (cf. Wilson, *Betjeman*, p. 159); 'tin' is slang for money (*OED*

3.a). When published in *The Betjemanian* the poem was not given a title, but Bevis Hillier reports that Betjeman's intention was that it be titled 'A Memory of 1940' (Hillier, *Bonus*, p. 238). I use as my copy-text the typescript in the John Murray Archives, the final version under consideration for publication in *High and Low*.

Aberdeen. Written in 1947. Preliminary typescript: McPherson Library Special Collections, University of Victoria. Written when Betjeman went to Aberdeen to research a BBC radio talk. The final version he sent on a postcard to a BBC producer, which was subsequently published in Candida Lycett Green, ed., *Letters, Volume One: 1926–1951*, p. 416. I use this version as my copy-text.

In Overcliffe. Written circa 1948–51 and published posthumously in Candida Lycett Green, ed., *Letters, Volume Two: 1951–1984*, p. 46. The poem was considered for inclusion in *A Few Late Chrysanthemums*, but late in 1953 Murray and Betjeman axed it from the galley proofs. We may never know how early the poem was written, but early drafts titled 'In Duncliffe' provide a hint that it may have been in the late 1940s. In 1948 Betjeman and four others signed a letter to *The Times* protesting the erection of wireless masts on Dorset hills; Duncliffe Hill was not threatened, but nearby Eggardon and Bulbarrow were. Another title considered for this poem was 'Adolescence' (cf. Peterson, *John Betjeman*, pp. 239, 425).

October Bells. Written circa 1949–50. Previously unpublished. Title supplied by the editor. Manuscript worksheets: McPherson Library Special Collections, University of Victoria. Poem reconstructed from three pages of well-developed drafts in an undated holograph notebook that also contains fourteen pages of notes of a trip to the Isle of Wight – probably for the 'Coast and Country' series, broadcast on BBC radio between 1949 and 1951. Two interesting variants: for line 7, 'Yellow shine the silent oaktops clustering in steel blue air'; for line 10, 'Dying, dying, dying, fruiting, all the reds and golds declare'.

The Corporation Architect. Published in *Harlequin* 2 (1950), p. 31. The poem refers to Sir Horace Jones, famed for designing Tower Bridge, but Betjeman takes some liberties with the facts of his life. In the documentary film *Time with Betjeman*, he reflects on Jones, who designed Smithfield Market near Betjeman's flat in Cloth Fair: 'He was the City Architect. He was a dear old thing. He was so fat that they had to carve a half-circle out of the council table in the RIBA in order to fit him in' (qtd. Hillier, *Bonus*, p. 534). For further details, see Candida Lycett Green, ed., *Letters, Volume One: 1926–1951*, p. 494.

The Weary Journalist. Published in 1950 in *Time and Tide*. It was included in *A Few Late Chrysanthemums* in 1954 but excluded from *Collected Poems* by Lord Birkenhead. Reprinted in Hillier, *New Fame*, p. 444. The poem satirizes the clichés trotted out in the earnest political editorials of *Time and Tide*, which Betjeman served as literary editor.

The Death of the University Reader of Spanish. Written in 1950, well before the actual death in 1958 of Betjeman's friend, the Oxford don George Alfred Magee Kolkhorst. In *Summoned by Bells*, Betjeman explains his nickname: 'We called you "Colonel" just because you were, / Though tall, so little like one' (p. 97). Magee was the surname of Kolkhorst's mother. Soda was his favourite dog. Fred and Souch were servants at Kolkhorst's Yarnton Manor. Dolly Trelease was an impoverished cousin who ran the house at Yarnton. Max Plowman (1883–1941) was a poet, pacifist and editor of the *Adelphi*, a literary journal published between 1923 and 1955. 'Honest TOBY' refers to the Oxford don Toby Strutt, a member of Kolkhorst's Beaumont Street salon in Oxford and a regular visitor to Yarnton. Father Hugh Bridle was a Church of Ireland clergyman. The poem was published posthumously in *The Betjemanian* 13 (2001–2), pp. 23–5, and was also printed in Candida Lycett Green, ed., *Letters, Volume One: 1926–1951*, p. 528.

A Curate for Great Kirkby. Written in 1953 to accompany a filmstrip for the Additional Curates Society. Previously unpublished and unrecorded. Typescript: University of Leeds, Brotherton Library, Elliott Collection. The script includes not only Betjeman's poem, divided into twenty-five sections corresponding to twenty-five frames of filmstrip, but also short descriptions of the scene in each frame and suggestions of 'patter' for the narrator to add to the poetic narrative Betjeman composed. His poem is so vivid that the filmstrip scene descriptions and patter are not essential except in three instances, where I have paraphrased and interpolated in brackets passages from the typescript's prose.

This poem has never been published, nor has it been recorded in any bibliographic inventory of Betjeman's writings. Peterson intentionally chose not to attempt to identify 'the film scripts he created for the Ministry of Information during the Second World War, [or the] one or more filmstrips that he produced for the SPCK', along with other ephemeral material such as advertising copy and blurbs for dust wrappers and record sleeves. Yet Peterson acknowledged that 'a surprising number of his poems were commissioned for radio and television programmes, and throughout his life Betjeman was eager to publish, whenever feasible, his scripts in book format' (Peterson, *John Betjeman*, xix–xx). To my knowledge the filmstrip itself is no longer extant, but we are fortunate that this remarkable and unusual poem is. Its survival is due to the sedulous collector Reg Read, who was one of Betjeman's closest companions in his final seven years. It was part of a cache of manuscripts put up for auction by Read's heirs, purchased by the University of Leeds and deposited in the Elliott Collection in the Brotherton Library.

'A Curate for Great Kirkby' bears many hallmarks of Betjeman's 'Poems in the Porch'. Considering that this piece was composed just before he started that series of radio poems, it seems plausible that the experience of writing voice-over poetry for a filmstrip taught him the essential skills necessary to create that collection of Anglican radio verse that commenced with 'Diary of a Church Mouse' in October 1953. The language and tone of 'A Curate for Great Kirkby' are remarkably similar to that of 'The Divine Society', a newly discovered 'Poem in the Porch' included here in *Harvest Bells*. Stanzas 18–20 in 'A Curate for Great Kirkby', where the vicar tricks Dad into helping with the building of the church and attending home church meetings, are the direct inspiration for the conversion of Emmanuel Seed in 'Advent Bells' (*Poems in the Porch: The Radio Poems of John Betjeman*, pp. 75–80).

I have no basis for believing that Betjeman wrote any of the prose passages that accompany this type-script. However, the suggested voice-over commentary for stanza 24 offers a simple Biblical theology that may speak less to the Church of England's practical need for curates than to Betjeman's Christian worldview: 'The Vicar starts to convert his people by first showing them how God works through history. Every nation that has put the state in the place of God has become a total loss to civilization. How God deals with one as an individual, his benefits to mankind unasked, the answer to prayer often so unobtrusive as to be unnoticed. All the benefits of this life, one's senses, friends, security, all gifts from God. Most important of all, he has given us our Lord Jesus Christ, the greatest gift of all.'

Clay and Spirit. Published in 1954 in *A Few Late Chrysanthemums* but excluded from *Collected Poems* by Lord Birkenhead. An early title, appearing on several manuscript and typescript drafts, was 'Autumn Clay'.

Not Necessarily Leeds. Published on 1 October 1954 in the *Spectator*. This poem was occasioned by the efforts of the Church of England in the 1950s to sell off churches deemed redundant. After the Bishop of London sold St Peter's, Great Windmill Street, Betjeman was determined to prevent further disaster, and in this poem he caustically attacks the Bishop of Ripon and the Archdeacon of Leeds for their plan to demolish Holy Trinity, Leeds, and sell off the land. Betjeman had already battled Archdeacon C. O. Ellison over the fate of Holy Trinity in a series of letters exchanged in the *Spectator* in 1954. Here, instead of defending the church on grounds of historic and architectural merit, Betjeman relies on a more powerful appeal – he attacks the bishop for following demographic trends instead of evangelizing. The bishop, motivated not so much by greed as by an obsession with financial stability, is all too happy to close an urban parish with declining attendance and create a united benefice if that will keep his budget in the black. Betjeman's attack on the bishop's apparent apathy to the spiritual needs of an urban, post-war people worked, and the church was not closed.

The St Paul's Appeal. Published on 27 October 1954 in *Punch* under the title 'Who Will Help St Paul's?' To reflect Betjeman's intentions, I have restored the original title as found in his typescripts and correspondence (British Library Add. MS 71935, ff. 202–5).

The Divine Society. Written circa 1956. Previously unpublished. Title supplied by the editor. Untitled typescript with minor holograph revisions: McPherson Library Special Collections, University of Victoria. This is a 'Poem in the Porch', designed to be read on BBC Radio in the 'Faith in the West' series. It exists in several holograph drafts as well as a final typescript; broadcast scripts, however, are not extant. I discovered this poem after my collection, *Poems in the Porch: The Radio Poems of John Betjeman*, was published in 2008. As I recounted in the Appendix of that book, two scheduled broadcasts of a 'Poem in the Porch' in 1956 I had been unable to identify – one in February, the other in December. Because Betjeman wrote to the producer in late November, 'I have been trying like anything to write for you, but I *can't* do this by December 7th. I really cannot' (Qtd. Peterson,

John Betjeman, p. 394), it seems likely that if Betjeman did read this poem on air, it was on 17 February 1956, the only remaining date for which a specific poem has not been identified with a known, scheduled broadcast. This is the only 'Poem in the Porch' I have selected for *Harvest Bells*; the others, though most are not in *Collected Poems*, are readily available in *Poems in the Porch: The Radio Poems of John Betjeman*, ed. Kevin Gardner (London: Continuum, 2008).

Village Wedding. Published on 11 July 1959 in the *New Yorker* and in the Winter 1959–1960 issue of *Cornhill*. Sally Weaver was the oldest and best friend of Betjeman's daughter, Candida. Candida and her father attended Sally's wedding together in Uffington in June 1958.

John Edward Bowle. Written circa 1960–1. Previously unpublished. Title supplied by the editor. Untitled holograph manuscript: McPherson Library Special Collections, University of Victoria. Multiple drafts are in the Victoria collection; the final version, in an undated notebook, is in a highly polished state with a few minor revisions. Some of the drafts are written on stationery from Edensor House, Derbyshire. This was the home of the Dowager Duchess of Devonshire, mother of Betjeman's mistress, Elizabeth Cavendish. Betjeman spent significant periods of time at Edensor House from the early 1950s through the early 1970s, but strong evidence points to a likely period of composition around 1960 or 1961. The poem is written in the imagined voice of John Edward Bowle, who was at Marlborough, then Oxford, with Betjeman. Although their relationship occasionally soured, they remained friends for life. A reunion of Old Marlburians in 1960, organized by Ben Bonas (who appears in the poem) and which Bowle and Betjeman both attended, may have been the occasion that inspired the poem. It bears significant narrative and thematic similarities with Betjeman's auto-biographical poem, 'Summoned by Bells' (1960), which further helps to date this poem, though the treatment of these elements here leans toward the satiric rather than the nostalgic. According to Candida Lycett Green, Bowle 'was interminably long-winded and took himself very seriously' (*Letters, Volume Two: 1951–1984*, p. 409), traits that must have tempted Betjeman sorely to tease him and to puncture his pomposity in this poem. It is difficult to gauge how Bowle might have reacted to Betjeman's satire. They worked together on the short-lived subversive school magazine at Marlborough, *The Heretick* (Hillier, *Young Betjeman*, p. 101), so Bowle surely had a taste for the satiric; whether that taste was sufficiently capacious to encompass self-deprecating laughter is unknown. Bowle held positions as history master at Westminster School and Eton College, was briefly a don at Wadham College, Oxford, then spent seventeen years on the faculty of the College of Europe in Bruges – a position he held at the time Betjeman wrote the poem. The lines are composed in loose, unrhymed dactylic hexameters with a medial caesura, a form Betjeman appro-priated from Longfellow's *Evangeline*.

1962. Written in 1962. Previously unpublished. Typescript: McPherson Library Special Collections, University of Victoria. Peterson notes that the poem was offered to the *New Yorker* in 1963 but was rejected (p. 440), perhaps because its satirical focus on civil servants and the honours system would confuse American readers. The speaker of the poem is unidentified, but it seems evident from his quotation of the Latin adage (meaning 'make haste slowly') and his assertion of having had a knighthood for forty years that he is sneering at the rapid advancement of civil servants up the social ladder.

Prologue Spoken by Peggy Ashcroft at the Opening of the Peggy Ashcroft Theatre, Croydon, 5 November 1962. Written in 1962. Previously unpublished. Holograph manuscripts and typescripts: McPherson Library Special Collections, University of Victoria. In their fascinating representation of the poetic process, the five surviving worksheets for this poem, together with two distinct fair copies and one typescript, would have delighted University of Buffalo librarian Charles Abbott. The poem exists in essentially two distinct final states: (a) a holograph fair copy in Betjeman's hand and a typescript, quite similar but with minor variants, of twenty-eight lines, and (b) a holograph fair copy in Peggy Ashcroft's hand, of twenty lines, with several individual lines significantly altered from the typescript and fair copy in Betjeman's hand. Surviving correspondence indicates that Ashcroft consulted with Betjeman, whom she had known and worked with since the early 1950s, about the poem and offered suggestions for revision. Betjeman would have trusted her views and, as she was the one to recite the poem, would likely have acceded to her wishes. I have therefore chosen the twenty-line version in her hand as copy-text, but I include the deleted stanzas here:

Ah! those balmy summer evenings when the Golden
    Rain would fall,

Twinkling as the organ thundered in the echoey
    central hall,
And the rockets dimmed the starshine of my child-
    hood's summer nights,
And that cliff of crystal glittered red to green in Bengal
    Lights.

Friendly were the streets of Croydon; leafy each
    suburban road
Round by Addiscombe and Wickham, calm prosper-
    ity's abode:
Bright the French Intensive Gardens near the Waddon
    Aerodrome
With their choice of rare Swiss Alpines for the rockery
    at home.

A Good Investment. Written circa 1963–4. Previously
unpublished. Title and initial edits courtesy of Bevis
Hillier. Untitled holograph manuscript: Beinecke Library,
Yale University. Only one draft of this poem is extant, in
an undated spiral notebook of drafts of poetry and prose.
The extant draft has a number of revisions, but it is in an
essentially final state. Minor editorial dilemmas are pres-
ent in lines 6–7 and 16–18; I have therefore adopted the
edits suggested in the transcription Bevis Hillier made
and kindly shared with me. The sequence of drafts in the
notebook, combined with external evidence, indicates that
1963–4 is the likeliest date of composition. In the notebook
it is preceded by multiple drafts of 'Beaumaris, December
21, 1963' and a fair copy draft of two stanzas of 'Caprice'.
It is followed by a draft of 'Archibald', very rough drafts
of three sections of *City of London Churches*, and a draft of
'Winter Seascape'. The first draft of 'Beaumaris' is undated

but the titular date of '21. 12. 63.' is added to the top of the third draft. Despite the December 1963 date, there is no evidence to suggest a correspondence between subtitle and composition. 'Beaumaris' was rejected for *High and Low* (1966) but included in *A Nip in the Air* (1974). 'Caprice' was written in 1956, so it seems likely that Betjeman returned to it at this time to consider revisions prior to publishing it in *High and Low*. The draft of 'Archibald' has no date, but considering that the final version was excluded from *High and Low* (it was eventually published in 1982 in *Uncollected Poems*), it seems likely that he was composing it at this time. *City of London Churches* was contracted in May 1962, and Betjeman worked on it through 1963 and 1964. 'Winter Seascape' is undated in this notebook, but another manuscript draft of this poem is on the same page as an early draft of the poem 'Autumn 1964' (McPherson Library Special Collections, University of Victoria).

St Mary's Chapel of Ease. Written in 1965 and included in a letter to John O'Dea. The poem describes Dublin's 'Black Church' off Parnell Square, a Church of Ireland edifice now deconsecrated. I use as my copy-text the holograph manuscript draft in the McPherson Library Special Collections, University of Victoria, John Betjeman Collection, MS PTO 046, which also includes Bejeman's sketch of the church. Candida Lycett Green edited and published the poem in *Letters, Volume Two: 1951–1984*, p. 285, but introduced some inexplicable variants, including the substitution in line three of 'the turf-smoke' for 'its silence': 'Which shall rise in the turf-smoke forbidding and dark'. Her explanation of difficult allusions is invaluable. 'Austin O' Clarke' is Austin Clarke, the poet who grew up in the shadow of the Black Church. 'Wilson' is Harold Wilson, the Prime Minister and a Methodist. 'McQuaid' is John Charles McQuaid, the Roman Catholic Archbishop of Dublin. 'Simms' is George Otto Simms, the Church of Ireland's Archbishop of Dublin. 'I.C.' is shorthand for Irish Catholic.

The Finest Work in England: I. K. Brunel. Written in 1966. Previously unpublished. Typescript with holograph revisions: McPherson Library Special Collections, University of Victoria. Betjeman wrote this poetic life of Isambard Kingdom Brunel as the script for a film documentary by Jonathan Stedall, *Footprints: The Finest Work in England*, which aired on BBC 2 on 15 May 1966 (cf. Peterson, *John Betjeman*, K107). Many of Betjeman's documentary scripts contain passages of original poetry, but a handful were done completely in verse. Two others worth seeking out are *Still Sidmouth* and *Marlborough*, both published in Stephen Games, ed., *Betjeman's England* (London: John Murray, 2009), pp. 97–101 and 269–73.

La Cometa Moraira. Probably written in 1967, perhaps as late as 1972. Previously unpublished. Holograph manuscript: McPherson Library Special Collections, University of Victoria. The poem appears in an undated spiralbound sketchbook and is accompanied by a watercolour painting of the scene described in the poem. Betjeman visited Spain in 1967, 1969, 1971 and 1972 (cf. Hillier, *Bonus*, pp. 317–18, 323–6). In 1967 and 1972 he stayed with friends in Moraira, where he most likely wrote this poem and painted the accompanying scene.

A Lament for Middlesex. Written in 1967. Title supplied by the editor. This poem is an extract from the script for *Contrasts: Marble Arch to Edgware – A Lament*, a film that premiered on BBC 1 on 31 January 1968. Betjeman wrote and recited four original poems for this documentary, but in my view this is the only one that works independently of the film itself. Stephen Games published Betjeman's summary film treatment of this documentary, which included all four poems together in a section of the film treatment titled 'Narrative' (*Betjeman's England*, pp. 157–64). 'Welsh Harp' is a local name for the Brent Reservoir in northwest London.

Castle Howard. Written in 1969. This poem is an extract from *Bird's-Eye View: The Englishman's Home*, a documentary film that premiered on BBC 2 on 5 April 1969. Betjeman wrote the script and provided the voice-over. The poem was resurrected for the script of *The Queen's Realm: A Prospect of England*, a documentary film that premiered on BBC 2 on 31 May 1977. The poem was published on 2 June 1977 in *The Listener*. For background on these films, see Hillier, *Bonus*, pp. 196–9, 448–9, and Lycett Green, ed., *Letters, Volume Two: 1951–1984*, pp. 360, 376–7.

Lines Read at the Wing Airport Resistance Movement Protest Meeting, June 1970. Published on 13 August 1970 in *The Times*, as a continuation of William Cowper's 1784 poem 'The Poplar Field'. The poem was reprinted in Lycett Green, ed., *Letters, Volume Two: 1951–1984*, p. 375, and in Hillier, *Bonus*, p. 274. Betjeman recited the poem at a large protest meeting in Oving, Buckinghamshire, on 20 June 1970. The airport was built at Stansted instead.

Sonnet. Published in 1973 in the novel *The Barrier* by Robin Maugham. This sonnet is the fourth of five that Maugham commissioned from Betjeman for his novel of interracial love in India. In my view it is the only one that works as a poem independent of the novel's context. The speaker of the sonnet is the novel's narrator – a white woman engaged in an adulterous love affair with a young Indian man.

Revenge. Written circa 1973–4. Previously unpublished. Typescript: McPherson Library Special Collections, University of Victoria. Typed on stationery headed with Betjeman's final London address, 29 Radnor Walk. He moved there in February 1973 and remained there for the rest of his life. It was a difficult adjustment at first, living in Chelsea. Bevis Hillier describes the scene as a 'Hieronymus Bosch pageant' and notes the 'sports-car engines being gunned and motor-bikes revving up in the small hours as young bloods left the Arethusa Club' (*Bonus*, p. 423). Although it is possible the poem was written later, its agitation with the noise of motorcycles points most likely to that first year or two of adjustment.

St Mary-le-Strand. Published in 1977 as a broadside when Betjeman helped to launch a campaign to raise funds for the church's restoration. For further details, see Hillier, *Bonus*, pp. 465–6. In addition to designing St Mary-le-Strand, James Gibbs (1682–1754) also designed St Martin-in-the-Fields, Oxford's Radcliffe Camera and Cambridge's Senate House.

My Landlady's Dog. Written in 1978. Title supplied by the editor. Untitled typescript: McPherson Library

Special Collections, University of Victoria. Typescript dated 15 January 1978. Hillier published an alternative version of this poem, with significant variants, titled 'A Dog Lover's Poem' (*Bonus*, p. 570). That version was inscribed by Betjeman on the flyleaf of a copy of *Archie and the Strict Baptists* and given to Peter Parker during a hospital convalescence in March 1978.

Guyhirn Chapel of Ease. Published in 1977 as a foreword to an historical and architectural pamphlet, *Guyhirn Chapel of Ease*, printed by the Redundant Churches Fund. Situated above the River Nene in Cambridgeshire, about fifteen miles east of Peterborough, this unadorned ecclesiastical structure was built in 1660 to Puritan tastes and worship practices. Its exterior is partly brick and partly stone; inside, its furnishings are austere, and its narrow pews are designed to prevent 'Popish' kneeling. Following the Restoration of Crown and Church that same year, and the Act of Uniformity two years later, the building was appropriated as a chapel of ease for the parish of Wisbech St Peter. It receives a brief mention in Betjeman's *Collins Guide to English Parish Churches* (1959) for its 'untouched Puritan simplicity' (p. 110). In 1973 Betjeman was appointed the first president of the Friends of Guyhirn Chapel of Ease. The building is now in the care of the Churches Conservation Trust.

St Bartholomew's Hospital. Published in the December 1978/January 1979 issue of *London Magazine*; reprinted in 1981 in *Church Poems*. In the *London Magazine* it is titled 'St Bartholomew's Hospital, EC1', though the postal code is not in the title of any of the drafts or typescripts, nor is it in the version printed in *Church Poems*. St Bartholomew's was founded as a hospital and priory in 1123 by Rahere, an Anglo-Norman monk and courtier of Henry I. In the shadow of the hospital stand the two churches, St Bartholomew the Less and St Bartholomew the Great. Betjeman was a parishioner of Great St Bart's when he lived across the street at 43 Cloth Fair from 1954 to 1973.

Who Took Away ... Published on 6 October 1979 in the *Spectator*. The poem laments the redrawing of the boundary lines between English counties and the renaming of historic place names. Avon and Humberside were created as non-metropolitan counties in 1974 and survived until a subsequent county restructuring in 1996. Thamesdown was a district of Wiltshire formed in 1974, subsequently renamed the Borough of Swindon.

Lines on the Unmasking of the Surveyor of the Queen's Pictures. Written in 1979. Published in *Private Eye* No. 469 (7 December 1969), p. 15, and attributed to 'The Poet Laureate Sir Jawn Bargeperson'. Holograph manuscript: McPherson Library Special Collections, University of Victoria. Handwritten note on manuscript, 'Put it in if you like it. It is not very good, is it? J.B.', is also reprinted at the end of the poem in *Private Eye*. The holograph contains minor variants in punctuation, capitalization and line indentation. The handwriting is not Betjeman's; by 1979 Parkinson's Disease had rendered his script almost entirely illegible. It is possible that the poem was copied out by his secretary, Elizabeth Moore, from dictation.

Anthony Blunt was Director of the Courtauld Institute and Surveyor of the Queen's Pictures. From the 1930s to the 1950s he was an active spy for the Soviet Union; a confession forced from him in 1965 was kept secret until 1979. The apparent insouciance of the poem's final stanza may be attributable to *Schadenfreude*. Although they had been close friends at Marlborough, Betjeman and Blunt had grown distant and their friendship had deteriorated by the 1950s, perhaps because Blunt made Betjeman feel that he had wasted his talents in pursuit of popularity (*Letters, Volume Two: 1951–1984*, p. 505). In 1968 Betjeman wrote to Lionel Perry, 'I saw Anthony Blunt yesterday and didn't speak. He always makes me feel trivial and shallow' (*Letters, Volume Two: 1951–1984*, p. 348).

Betjeman's use of the phrase 'nine-day wonder', a proverbial expression which refers to a short-lived sensation or something that becomes boring after nine days, cleverly turns the charge of triviality back on Blunt. The phrase 'straining at a gnat' alludes to the Gospel of Matthew, in which Jesus is exposing the hypocrisy of the scribes and Pharisees in a vitriolic assault: 'Ye blind guides, which strain at a gnat, and swallow a camel' (Matthew 23:24). These allusions reveal that Betjeman's tone is far from flippant, though his nonchalance partly masks the charges of hypocrisy and triviality. In this sense, Betjeman replicates the unmasking of Blunt in the exposure of his own subconscious feelings, which lurk behind a typical Betjemanesque facade of moral and aesthetic superficiality.

Whether intentionally or unintentionally, Betjeman commits two errors: the river that Betjeman would have recalled seeing Blunt walk beside at Marlborough was the Kennet, not the Talbot; and Blunt did not retire to Maida Vale (which had once been home to Kim Philby) but rather to a flat near the Courtauld Institute. Betjeman's derisive comment about Blunt's sexuality may have been accurate: 'the reality [of his sex life] was unequal partners and a lot of rough trade', as Julian Barnes has noted ('Enigma', *The New Yorker*, 14 January 2002).

Dawlish. Published in 1983 in a limited-edition exhibition guide titled *A Catalogue of Works by Sir John Betjeman from the Collection of Ray Carter in the Art Gallery of St Paul's School February–March MCMLXXXIII*. The poem is dedicated to 'MW' – perhaps Mary Wilson, wife of the prime minister, Harold Wilson, who had befriended Betjeman in 1967. I have been unable to discover any details about the poem's date of composition, though some of its language ('Down here', 'those panes') indicates that it might be an extract from an unidentified television documentary, perhaps a passage rejected from the script for *Beside the Seaside*, a documentary film in the 'Bird's-Eye View' series, broadcast on BBC 2 in 1969.

APPENDIX A:
A PORTUGUESE TRANSLATION

'Mar Português'
Fernando Pessoa (1888–1935)

Ó mar salgado, quanto do teu sal
são lágrimas de Portugal!
Por te cruzarmos, quantas mães choraram,
quantos filhos em vão rezaram!
Quantas noivas ficaram por casar
para que fosses nosso, ó mar!

Valeu a pena? Tudo vale a pena
se a alma não é pequena.
Quem quer passar além do Bojador
tem que passar além da dor.
Deus ao mar o perigo e o abismo deu,
mas nele é que espelhou o céu.

'Portuguese Sea'

[LITERAL TRANSLATION]

O salty sea, how much of your salt is tears of Portugal!
How many mothers wept, how many sons prayed in vain,
that we might cross you! How many maidens remained
unmarried, that you might be ours, o sea!

Was it worth while? All is worth while if the soul is
not small. He who wishes to pass beyond the Cape must

pass beyond pain. God gave the sea the danger and the abyss, but it is in it that the heaven is mirrored.

[FREE TRANSLATION]

> O sea, how much of thy sharp salt
> Is tears from Portugal!
> That we might cross you, many mothers wept,
> The prayers of many sons were vain!
> How many maidens ever lonely slept
> That thou mightest be ours, o main!
>
> Was the pain worth it? All is worth the pain
> If only the soul scorns the mean.
> Who longs beyond the Cape to pass
> Must beyond anguish also pass.
> God gave the sea both danger and abyss
> But there it is that heaven mirrored lies.

[FINAL FORM]

> O sea, how much of your salt
> Is sharp with the tears of Portugal?
> How many mothers have wept
> And sons prayed vainly to cross you
> And maidens remained unmarried
> That we might claim you as our own
> O salty seas of Portugal.
>
> And was the price too high?
> Not if the soul can pay it
> Not if the soul is big enough
> To round the cape and discover
> Further perils beyond,

For God who created the waters
Made them also mirror his heaven.

Note. Translated in 1973. Never before published.
Manuscripts and typescripts: McPherson Library Special
Collections, University of Victoria. One of Betjeman's
earliest and most successful commissions as Poet Laureate
is his translation of Fernando Pessoa's 'Mar Português' as
'Portuguese Sea', set to music by Arthur Bliss, Master of
the Queen's Music. It was composed for and performed
at a 1973 state dinner attended by the prime ministers
of Portugal and the United Kingdom, celebrating the
six-hundredth anniversary of the Anglo-Portuguese
Alliance (Peterson, *John Betjeman*, p. 320). The versions
of the texts above exist in typescript. The extent to which
Betjeman was involved in the 'literal' translation above
is uncertain. Three surviving holograph manuscripts in
Betjeman's hand suggest that the 'free' and 'final' versions
are entirely Betjeman's. I leave it to a future music histo-
rian to recover Bliss's musical manuscripts.

APPENDIX B:
A POSSIBLE ATTRIBUTION

FRÖHLICHES WEIHNACHTEN:
VON DER P-VSN-RREISE

From heart of Mittel Europe
   I make der little trip
to show those Englisch dummkopfs
   some echtdeutsch Scholarship.
Viel Sehenswürdigkeiten[1]
   by others have been missed,
but now comes to enlighten
   der Great Categorist.

Der Georgian und Viktorian
   ist so-wie-so 'getan'[2]
bei Herr Professor Richardtson
   und Dichter Betjemann.
While oders gifs you Stevenage,
   Stonehenge und Gilbert Scott,
From Pleiocene to C.19
   I gifs der blooming lot!

Zu jeder Church in London[3]
   ich schoss in froher Eil[4]
und hab' schon 'was gefunden[5]
   im echt Rundbogen-style.[6]

'So beefy und ham-fisted'
  ich hatt' ein damgoodlook,
but soon es war gelisted
  in meinem Penguinbuch.

Ich ging einmal nach Ealing[7]
  – ach wie ein schönes Dorf![8]
to list a Georgian ceiling
  restored by Edward Maufe.
Und dann sofort nach Morden[9]
  im Auto I did scorch
to note a church by Porden
  with 'veryrumcurved porch'.

To go out 'on the bendl'[10]
  ach, das ist wunderschön!
mit Herrn Goodhart-Rendel
  und Johann Sommersohn.
Gross Scott! But we are noisy
  und have such Lustigkeit,[11]
we can't distinguish Voysey
  from Temple Moore or Tite.

I fly across the Atlantik
  and talk both day and night
on Baukunst and the Antik[12]
  and style of Franklloydwright.
Till Hitchcock cries: 'Quit stoogin',
  it ain't no doggone good
to call Augustus Pugin
  a chip off Sancton Wood.'

Once on perambulation
    I walk twelve miles or more
to note an elevation
    in style of Norman Shaw.
The rooms were full of dampness,
    the cellars full of mice.
I note: 'Perhaps by Champneys,
    not specially nice.'

All rest shall be resisted
    till every stone and brick
is finally gelisted
    by Herr Professor N-k.
Mit broadcast, book and Lektur
    rolls in der £.s.d.
Der British Architektur –
    Ach, dat's der game for me!

Glosses

1 *Viel Sehenswürdigkeiten*: Many attractions, things
   worth seeing
2 *ist so-wie-so 'getan'*: is anyhow over, done
3 *Zu jeder Church in London*: At any church in London
4 *ich schoss in froher Eil*: I dart about in joyful haste; see
   Note for further information
5 *und hab' schon 'was gefunden*: and have already found it
6 *im echt Rundbogen-style*: in true round-arched style
7 *Ich ging einmal nach Ealing*: I once went to Ealing
8 *ach wie ein schönes Dorf*: oh what a lovely village
9 *Und dann sofort nach Morden*: And then immediately
   after [to] Morden

10 *on the bendl*: on a bender; see Note for further infor-
mation
11 *Lustigkeit*: merriment, jolly times
12 *Baukunst and the Antik*: architecture and antiquities

Note. Written circa 1953. Typescript: Noel Blakiston Papers,
Eton College Collections. First printed in Hillier, *Bonus*, pp.
45–6, 636–7. Having been shown a copy of the poem by Ian
Grant, an architect and the secretary to the Victorian Society,
Hillier attributed the poem's authorship to Peter Clarke,
Assistant Secretary of *The Times* and, along with Grant,
Betjeman and Pevsner, a founding member of the Victorian
Society. Clarke published a number of related satirical squibs
and parodies (cf. Hillier, *Bonus*, pp. 29–31, 43–6).

Despite Hillier's attribution to Clarke, there is strong
evidence the poem may be by Betjeman. The typescript
in the Blakiston Papers at Eton has Betjeman's name
inscribed in hand (apparently by Noel Blakiston) and is
accompanied by a letter from Noel's widow, Georgiana,
dated 9 November 1991, to the Eton College archivist. In
it she explains why she came to believe that her husband
was correct in attributing the poem to Betjeman: 'In spite
of Noel's note at the bottom of the page I had my doubts
about this, but Elizabeth Cavendish confirms that it is
by John Betjeman and she remembers him writing it. It
was never published as it was considered to be libelous.
She tells me John absolutely loathed Pevsner. I am glad it
should be among Noel's papers at Eton.'

Internal evidence of authorship is no less confusing. Its
jokes at Pevsner's expense bear little resemblance to other
things Betjeman had said about Pevsner in print from the
1930s through the 1950s, much of which is extraordinarily

vitriolic and humourless. In tone, this piece is more in tune with Hillier's assessment of Clarke's sense of humour: 'it amused him, in his slightly feline way, to play on John's dislike of Pevsner' (*Bonus*, p. 49). The poem's rhythms are distinctly Betjeman's, but Clarke was known to be a skilled mimic, so that indicates nothing. Betjeman had no felicity with languages, yet he enjoyed linguistic wordplay immensely, and his letters are full of such joking.

In the end, authorship cannot be determined satisfactorily. Giana Blakiston's report that Elizabeth Cavendish distinctly remembered Betjeman writing the poem is impossible to dismiss. Yet unless further evidence arises, this poem should be considered only possibly written by Betjeman. Based on the strong but conflicting evidence provided by Bevis Hillier and Giana Blakiston, I am inclined to consider the piece a collaborative effort between Betjeman and Clarke.

The poem is highly allusive. In l. 8 the nickname for Pevsner, the 'Great Categorist', was first applied to Aristotle. In l. 18 is an echo of the second line of 'Die Forelle' ('The Trout'), a poem by Christian Schubart and set to music by Franz Schubert: 'Da schoss in froher Eil'; Hillier asserts (*Bonus*, p. 45) that the poem was designed to be sung to Schubert's melody. In l. 24, 'Penguinbuch' alludes to the fact that Pevsner's *Buildings of England* series was first published by Penguin. In l. 32, 'very-rumcurved porch' comically echoes Pevsner's description of the Tate Library, South Lambeth Road, as having a 'rum curved porch' (*London*, p. 275). Finally, the phrases 'not specially nice' (l. 56) and 'So beefy und ham-fisted' (l. 21) were used by Peter Clarke in a parody of Pevsner published in *Punch* in 1954 (qtd. Hillier, p. 29).

The phrase 'on the bendl' in the first line of the fifth stanza poses an interpretive dilemma. The Eton College typescript of the poem has quotation marks around the phrase, perhaps to indicate that it is a joke or pun, while the version printed by Hillier in *Bonus* uses only a single apostrophe at the end of *bendl*, suggesting that the word has been truncated. The context would seem to call for *offener Strasse* or *reisen* or (considering the implications of 'noisy' and 'Lustigkeit') *Sauftour* – except that a word was needed to rhyme with 'Rendel'. I believe that 'bendl' is a Teutonicized nonsense word meant to suggest a 'bender'.

Architects named or referenced in the poem: Albert Richardson (1880–1964), Sir Gilbert Scott (1811–78), Edward Maufe (1882–1974), William Porden (1755–1822), Harry Stuart Goodhart-Rendel (1887–1959), C. F. A. Voysey (1857–1941), Temple Moore (1856–1920), William Tite (1798–1873), Frank Lloyd Wright (1867–1959), Henry-Russell Hitchcock (1903–87), Augustus Pugin (1812–52), Sancton Wood (1815–86), Norman Shaw (1831–1912) and Basil Champneys (1842–1935). 'Johann Sommersohn' is a Teutonicizing of John Summerson (1904–92), the noted architectural historian.

In explaining why the poem was not published in her letter to the Eton archivist, Giana Blakiston says it was considered 'libellous'. In this she appears to concur with Hillier, who writes that 'It was considered too scabrous to publish but was gleefully circulated among Victorian Society members and others, some of whom assumed that John was its author' (*Bonus*, p. 45). With the passage of more than sixty years since its composition, it no longer seems terribly vicious or remotely libellous but rather jesting and playful. According to Hillier, Pevsner did not mind being the butt of these jokes and parodies (*Bonus*, p. 30), so there seems little reason for the poem to have been suppressed.

A NOTE ON THE AUTHOR

Sir John Betjeman was born in 1906 and educated at Marlborough and Magdalen College, Oxford. He gave his first radio talk in 1932; future appearances made him into a national celebrity. He was knighted in 1969 and appointed poet laureate in 1972. He died in 1984.

Dr Kevin J. Gardner is Professor of English at Baylor University, USA. The author of many articles and books, he is the editor of *Poems in the Porch, Building Jerusalem* and *Faith and Doubt of John Betjeman*.